College Teacher Training

College Teacher Training

Ajoy Chatterjee

CRESCENT
PUBLISHING CORPORATION

[The responsibility for the facts stated, conclusions reached and plagiarism, if any, in this book is entirely that of the Author. And the Publisher bears no responsibility for them, whatsoever.]

College Teacher Training

Edition : 2018

ISBN 81-8342-055-9

Published by:

CRESCENT PUBLISHING CORPORATION
4806/24, Mathur Lane,
Ansari Road, Darya Ganj,
New Delhi - 110002
Ph.: 011-23244131
Mob.: 9711991838, 9999021668
e-mail : crescentbook@gmail.com
Website : www.crescentpublishingcorp.weebly.com

Printed at :
Balaji Digital
Delhi

Preface

Teacher training is the professional preparation of teachers, usually through formal course work and practice teaching. Although the concept of teaching as a profession is fairly new, most teachers in industrialised nations today are college or university educated. The amount of preparatory training, however, varies greatly worldwide. Certification requirements for teaching have advanced with educational opportunity, although they vary widely from country to country. The trend in certification has been toward requiring more complete training, with practice teaching and extensive graduate work for specialised positions.

In many countries extension or summer graduate work is required of teachers or is made a prerequisite for advancement. A number of graduate professional degrees are now offered, including the Master of Arts in Teaching and the Doctor of Education. While the professional requirements for teaching have in the past stressed method and psychology, increasing emphasis is now being placed on subject-matter specialisation. Improvements in teacher training led to demands for professional recognition and benefits. These resulted in the formation of several international organisations as well as local and national teachers' unions.

This book comprehensively describes the problems and methods of college teacher training. It is divided into eight chapters. It is hoped that this book will prove useful to the teaching departments and institutions, teachers of educational administrations as well.

Ajoy Chatterjee

Contents

1

Principles of Teacher Training

Someone has not taught unless someone else has learned. After a few years of teaching, many faculty realize that students learn too little of what they teach. Science teaching requires attention to both the content of the course and the process of moving students from their initial state of knowledge and understanding to the desired level. In fact, teaching is part of a whole that comprises the teacher, the learner, the disciplinary content, the teaching/learning process, and the evaluation of both the teacher and the learner. Undergraduate students value good teaching, and many of those who switch from a science major to another field cite poor teaching as an important factor in their decision. When the data from students who persist in a science major was combined with data from students who switched out of a science major, poor teaching by science faculty was the students' most frequently cited concern.

Although students are turned off by poor teaching, they also have identified characteristics of good teaching:

- a teacher's enthusiasm and passion for the subject,
- rapport between a teacher and a student or group of students during discussions in and out of class,

- intellectual challenges from a teacher,
- clarity and organization in presenting analytical and conceptual understanding of ideas, and
- a teacher's scholarship.

Methods of Teaching

Recent research indicates that teachers teach in a manner consistent with their own way of learning . However, it is not necessarily true that student learning can be understood from the teachers' own learning history. What is your style of learning? Do you learn most easily if material is presented to you in a formal and structured manner, or do you learn most easily if you are forced to discover basic principles from a series of exercises and examples? Do you believe that your students will learn best if you use a teaching style that helped you learn as a student? Studies of teaching and learning have led to classification of teaching styles into three general categories: discipline-centered, instructor-centered, and student-centered. In discipline-centered teaching, the course has a fixed structure.

The needs, concerns, and requirements of teacher and student are not considered because the course is driven by and depends mainly on the disciplinary content that must be presented. The teacher transmits information, but the content is dictated by some separate authority such as a department syllabus committee or textbook author.

The teacher acts as a model of the educated person in instructor-centered teaching. He or she is regarded as the authoritative expert, the main source of knowledge, and the focal point of all activity. The student is the passive recipient of the information already acquired by the teacher. The teacher selects from the discipline the information to be taught, studied, and learned. Student-centered teaching focuses on the student and, in particular, on the cognitive development of the student.

The teacher's goal is to help students grasp the development of knowledge as a process rather than a product. The focus of classroom activities and assignments is on the student-centered process of inquiry itself, not on the products of inquiry. Students create their own conceptual or cognitive models. Content, teaching style, and methods are adapted to aid the cognitive and intellectual growth of students.

Student-centered teaching combines an under-standing of the way that humans process information with other factors that affect learning such as attitudes, values, beliefs, and motivation.

Although there are many ways to teach effectively, all require that the teacher have knowledge of three things:

1) the material being taught;
2) the best instructional strategies to teach the material; and
3) how students learn.

New faculty members typically know far more about the content of their discipline than they do about instructional strategies, and therefore tend to use teaching styles similar to those used by their own teachers. In most cases, they use elements of all three general teaching styles. As the teacher gains experience, his or her teaching style is likely to change. The first step in preparing to teach a particular course is to decide on a particular style of teaching that is compatible with and appropriate for your students and the goals of your course. It is likely that you will use a combination of the three teaching styles, depending on the circumstances of your course.

While developing their own teaching style, science teachers must answer a fundamental question: Is the primary goal of my course for each student to gain specific information, or for each student to master how to organize and apply new information independently to new situations? The primary goal may not be the same for each student in a course, especially when the students come from diverse backgrounds.

In courses that are the foundation for more advanced learning in a subject area, how should the content be organized and presented? Because science curricula tend to be vertically structured, students' content knowledge is critical for advancement in a field and for understanding the next level of information. In science courses for nonscience majors, how should the content be organized and presented? In any given course, we should ask what should be the balance between specific information, application of that information, and conceptual understanding of basic principles? If the course is truly to be a course for lawyers, citizens, teachers, and other nonscientists, it should provide some of the essence of what science is and the nature of the scientific enterprise.

Syllabus Design

Some faculty members find it useful to meet with their colleagues to design a syllabus that optimizes the order and structure in which to present the course material. For example, if you are teaching atomic theory, is it best to start with basic terms and then to build up to a model, or to start with a model and disassemble it piece by piece? The first step in collaborative syllabus design is to meet with fellow faculty members who teach the same course to identify basic concepts. Then, separately, each teacher does an analysis of the critical variables related to each concept. Finally, the colleagues reassemble to compare their lists, identify similarities and differences, and discuss the implications of their lists for instruction. Most science courses, particularly introductory courses, emphasize discipline-centered teaching. Generations of students have been exposed to science as a subject in which the correct formulas and answers must be memorized, and the material is divided into many different and seemingly unrelated pieces. Problems with this approach have been exacerbated by the explosion of scientific information. Faculty members, wishing to cover the latest results and ideas but reluctant to discard classical material, rush to cover more and more information in the same amount of time.

Instructor-centered and student-centered teaching are more effective than is discipline centered teaching for students to learn in this way. When the focus is on meaning rather than solely on facts, students develop their conceptual abilities. They assimilate information by incorporating new concepts or by using information to differentiate among already existing concepts. This is not necessarily at the expense of their development of algorithmic abilities, because conceptual understanding gives a context for the application of problem-solving methods.

A student-centered style is more likely to motivate students by engaging their interest. Several factors can influence your choice of teaching style:

— student needs (future course and career requirements, preparation for participatory citizenship, and preparation for careers in science, engineering, technology, or education),

- student background,
- familiarity with various teaching methods,
- course enrollment (size, students with special needs, the logistics of managing small group activities),
- student learning styles,
- teaching load (number of contact hours, office hours, time for preparation and grading),
- other responsibilities (research, committee work, administrative duties),
- support structures (equipment cost, teaching and demonstration asistants),
- facilities (laboratory equipment and computers, classroom and laboratory space, and demonstration equipment), and
- parallel sections that require some uniformity of coverage and examination.

Time constraints, class size, or course goals may lead to an emphasis on factual knowledge at the expense of developing a conceptual framework. Students are usually encouraged to accept facts from some authority (e.g., the instructor or the text) without questioning. If all their learning is rote learning, however, students seldom associate the new facts with concepts or models already part of their pictures of the world. How teachers teach is influenced to a great degree by what they teach and by how their courses are organized.

The usual focus in organizing a course is the content. A syllabus typically includes the organization of topics into an outline of the course of study, readings, exercises, examinations, and grading scheme. These features are important, but it is equally important to identify the goals of the course and to work both forward and backward to develop your syllabus. Student behaviors such as developing abilities to work in groups might also be included. Daniel D. Perlmutter of the University of Pennsylvania has developed a course called "Perspectives on Energy and the Environment." The goal of this course, which was taught for the first time in the 1994-1995 school year, is to provide nonscience majors with a quantitative understanding of science and technology.

The course fulfills the University's Physical Science requirement and is open to students who are not science, math, or engineering majors. It emphasizes applications to current energy and environmental issues and focuses on techniques and approaches to problem solving. Men and women who do not have professional interests in science and engineering still need to become informed in these areas in order to function effectively in a complex world.

The material draws heavily upon information from recent news reports on subjects having to do with energy or environmental matters. In each case the technical and policy issues are summarized and where appropriate brief calculations check the assertions of the reporter or experts cited in the article. Having seen such examples, the student will be sensitized to the relevant scientific questions that bear on an issue, and may recognize how technical limitations on what is or is not possible can form bases for preliminary judgments on the merits of a controversy. Most important of all, when information is lacking for a full assessment to be made, the student will have a framework for asking appropriate questions that can serve to elicit the necessary additional details.

Research on how students learn science offers three fundamental guide lines for course design:

- Become aware of the students' prior knowledge and take it into account.
- Identify the major and minor concepts and the connections between different concepts.
- Relate new information to a context the student understands. Along with repetition and application, these relationships are extremely important for student retention of the material.

To achieve these goals, a syllabus might include the following:

- overview of the course's purpose, including a rationale for why students should learn the material,
- the learning goals or objectives (what students should know or be able to do after completing the course),
- the conceptual structure used to organize the course,
- the important topics covered by the course,
- sequencing of topics so that major concepts are introduced early and can be reinforced through application to new situations,
- identification of the methods and accuracy of inquiry used to develop concepts and to identify the major information of the field,
- important knowledge, skills, or experience students need to succeed in the course, and
- evaluation and feedback strategies.

Student learning is enhanced when we are able to help students see the relationships among the sciences, and between science and mathematics, the humanities, social sciences, and the arts. Organizing courses around themes, issues, or projects not only can broaden student thinking and problem-solving abilities, but also can enrich the students' view of science as a multi faceted enterprise. Many lament the quality of science education for children in elementary, middle, and high schools, yet all precollege teachers were once under graduates, and almost all teachers took introductory science classes to learn about the science they now must teach. In physics, standard lectures do not help most students develop conceptual understanding of fundamental processes in electricity and in mechanics. Similarly, student grades in a large general chemistry lecture course do not correlate with the lecturing skills and experience of the instructor.

Despite the limitations of traditional lectures, many institutions are forced to offer high-enrollment introductory science courses. Many professors who teach these courses feel that lecturing is their only option, and can only dream of what they could accomplish in smaller classes. However, there is a small but growing group of science faculty members who have developed ways to engage students in the process of thinking, questioning, and problem solving despite the large class size. Strategies in use in introductory courses in biology and geology are described in the sidebars. Although many of the methods described in these sidebars are consistent with what experts know about how students learn, they may not be welcomed by all of the students in a class. There are several ways to help students make the transition from passive listeners to active participants in their own learning:

– Start off slowly; students may not have much experience in active learning.

- Introduce change at the beginning of a course, rather than midway through.
- Avoid giving students the impression that you are "experimenting" with them.

Effective Lecturing Method

Calling on individual students to answer questions or offer comments can also hold student attention; however, some students prefer a feedback method with more anonymity. If they have an opportunity to discuss a question in small groups, the group can offer an answer, which removes any one student from the spotlight. Another option is to have students write their answer on an index card, and pass the card to the end of the row; the student seated there can select one answer to present, without disclosing whose it is. The literature on teaching and learning contains other examples of techniques to maintain students' attention in a lecture setting:

- Avoid direct repetition of material in a textbook so that it remains a useful alternative resource.
- Use paradoxes, puzzles, and apparent contradictions to engage students.
- Make connections to current events and everyday phenomena.
- Begin each class with something familiar and important to students.
- End each class by summarizing the main points you have made.
- Adopt a reasonable and adjustable pace that balances content coverage and student understanding.

Consider using slides, videos, films, CD-ROMs, and computer simulations to enhance presentations, but remember that:

- Students cannot take notes in darkened rooms.
- The text needs to be large enough to read from the back of the room.
- Students need time to summarize their observations and to draw and note conclusions.

Pay attention to delivery:

- Maintain eye contact with students in all parts of the room.
- Step out from behind the lecture bench when feasible.
- Move around, but not so much that it is distracting.
- Talk to the students, not the blackboard.
- If using the board, avoid blocking it with AV projectors or screens.
- Shift the mood and intensity.
- Vary presentation techniques.

At the beginning of a course, discuss with your students several strategies for effectively engaging in and learning from your classes. Some may just listen, others will take notes, and still others may try to transcribe your words. Some students may want to tape the class session. If you want to encourage a particular form of student participation, make clear your expectations, the reasons for them, and how students' learning will benefit.

Whether in lecture, discussion sections, laboratories, or individual encounters, questioning is an important part of guiding students' learning. When students ask questions, they are often seeking to shortcut the learning process by getting the right answer from an authority figure. However, it is the processes of arriving at an answer and assessing the validity of an answer that are usually more important, particularly if the student can apply these processes to the next question. Both of these processes are obscured if the teacher simply gives the requested answer. Often, the Socratic method—meeting a student's question with another question—forces students (while often frustrating them) to offer possible answers, supporting reasons, and assessments.

In fact, posing questions can be an effective teaching technique. Here are some tips for the effective use of questions:

- Wait long enough to indicate that you expect students to think before answering. Some students know that if they are silent the professor will give the answer.
- Solicit the answer from a volunteer or a selected student.
- Determine the student's confidence level as you listen to the answer.
- Solicit alternative answers or elaboration to provide material for comparison, contrast, and assessment.
- Solicit additional responses from the same students with a leading question or follow-up observation.
- Direct the ensuing discussion to the comparison, evaluation, and extension of the offered answers rather than simple validation or refutation of right and wrong answers.
- Pose a second or follow-up question to continue the exploration.

Demonstrations can be very effective for illustrating concepts in class, but can result in passive learning without careful attention to engaging students. They can provoke students to think for themselves and are especially helpful if the demonstration has a surprise, challenges an assumption, or illustrates an otherwise abstract concept or mechanism. Demonstrations that use everyday objects are especially effective and require little preparation on the part of faculty. Students' interest is peaked if they are asked to make predictions and vote on the most probable outcome. There are numerous resources available to help faculty design and conduct demonstrations.

Many science education periodicals contain one or more demonstrations in each issue. The "Tested Demonstrations" column in the Journal of Chemical Education and the "Favorite Demonstration" column in the Journal of College Science Teaching are but two of the many examples. The American Chemical Society and the University of Wisconsin Press have published excellent books on chemical demonstrations. Similar volumes of physics demonstrations have been published by the American Association of Physics Teachers.

You should consider a number of issues when planning a demonstration:

- What concepts do you want the demonstration to illustrate?
- Which of the many demonstrations on the selected topic will generate the greatest enhancement in student learning?
- Where in the class would it be most effective?

- What prior knowledge should be reviewed before the demonstration?
- What design would be most effective, given the materials at hand and the target audience?
- Which steps in the demonstration procedure should be carried out ahead of time?
- What questions will be appropriate to motivate and direct student observation and thought processes before, during, and after the demonstration?
- What follow-up questions can be used to test and stretch students' understanding of the new concept?
- If the classroom or lecture hall is large, consider whether students in the back will be able to see your demonstration. Look into videotaping the demonstration and projecting the image on a larger screen so that all of your students can see.

Small group discussion sections often are used in large-enrollment courses to complement the lectures. In courses with small enrollments, they can substitute for the lecture, or both lecture and discussion formats can be used in the same class period. The main distinction between lecture and discussion is the level of student participation that is expected, and a whole continuum exists. Discussions can be instructor-centered (students answer the instructor's questions) or student-centered. In any case, discussion sessions are more productive when students are expected to prepare in advance. Focused discussion is an effective way for many students to develop their conceptual frameworks and to learn problem-solving skills as they try out their own ideas on other students and the instructor. The give and take of technical discussion also sharpens critical and quantitative thinking skills.

Classes in which students must participate in discussion force them to go beyond merely plugging numbers into formulas or memorizing terms. They must learn to explain in their own words what they are thinking and doing. Students are more motivated to prepare for a class in which they are expected to participate actively. However, student-centered discussions are less predictable than instructor-centered presentations, they are more time consuming, and they can require more skill from the teacher. To lead an effective discussion, the teacher must be a good facilitator, by ensuring that key points are covered and monitoring the group dynamics. Guidance is needed to keep the discussion from becoming disorganized or irrelevant.

Some students do not like or may not function effectively in a class where much of the time is devoted to student discussion. Some may take the point of view that they have paid to hear the expert (the teacher). For them, and for all students, it is useful to review the benefits of discussion-based formats in contrast with lectures whose purpose is to transmit information. Sensitivity to personality, cultural, linguistic, and gender differences that may affect students' participation in discussions is also important, especially if participation is graded. When students do not spontaneously engage in a discussion, they may be unprepared or they may be reluctant to speak or to be assertive. Some may be more comfortable making comparisons than absolute statements, and others may be more comfortable with narrative descriptions than with quantitative analysis. You might try various strategies to engage your students in meaningful discussion by posing questions that measure different levels of understanding.

Probably the best overall advice is to be bold but flexible and willing to adjust your strategies to fit the character of your class. If you want to experiment with using discussions in your class, here are some things to consider: Decide on the goals of your class,discussion. What is it that you want the students to get from each class session? Concepts? Problem solving skills? Decision-making skills? The ability to make connections to other disciplines or to technology? Broader perspective? Keep in mind that the goals may change as you progress through the material during the quarter or semester. Explain to the students how discussions will be structured.

Will the discussion involve the whole class or will students work in smaller groups? Make clear what you expect them to do before coming to each class session: read the chapter, think about the questions at the end of the chapter, seriously try to do the first five problems, etc. Students who do not come to class may not be studying. If you want students to discuss questions and concepts in small groups, explain to students how the groups will form. Do not allow a few students to dominate the discussion. Some students will naturally respond more quickly, but they must be encouraged to let others have a chance. Be sure that all students participate at an acceptable level. In extreme cases you may have to speak outside of class to an aggressive or an excessively reticent student. Look for opportunities for you or your students to bring to class mini-demonstrations illustrating important points of the day's topic.

This is a very effective way to stimulate discussion. Be willing to adjust to the needs of your students and to take advantage of your own strengths as a teacher. Watch for signs that the students need more or less guidance. Are the main points coming out and getting resolved? Do you need to do more summarizing or moderating? Collaborative learning "is an umbrella term for a variety of educational approaches involving joint intellectual effort by students, or students and teachers together". Cooperative learning, a form of collaborative learning, is an instructional technique in which students work in groups to achieve a common goal, to which they each contribute in individually accountable ways. The interaction itself can take different forms:

- out-of-class study groups
- in-class discussion groups
- project groups (in and/or out of class)
- groups in which roles (leader, timekeeper, technician, spokesperson, and so forth) are assigned and rotated

Although cooperative learning has been used effectively in elementary, middle, and high schools for a number of years, as discussed by Johnson and Johnson and Slavin, few studies have been done to demonstrate its effectiveness in the college classroom. Nevertheless, a growing number of practitioners are assessing its effectiveness). While many advocates of collaborative learning are quick to point out its advantages, they are also sensitive to its perceived problems. Cooper, for example, points out that coverage, lack of control during class, and students who do not carry their weight in a group, need to be considered before embarking on collaborative learning.

Laboratories

Experimentation underlies all scientific knowledge and understanding. Laboratories are wonderful settings for teaching and learning science. They provide students with opportunities to think about, discuss, and solve real problems. Developing and teaching an effective laboratory requires as much skill, creativity, and hard work as proposing and executing a first-rate research project. Despite the importance of experimentation in science, introductory labs fail to convey the excitement of discovery to the majority of our students. They generally give introductory science labs low marks, often describing them as boring or a waste of time. What is wrong? It is clear that many introductory laboratory programs are suffering from neglect. Typically, students work their way through a list of step-by-step instructions, trying to reproduce expected results and wondering how to get the right answer. While this approach has little do with science, it is common practice because it is efficient. Laboratories are costly and time consuming, and predictable, "cookbook" labs allow departments to offer their lab courses to large numbers of students. Improving undergraduate laboratory instruction has become a priority in many institutions, driven, in part, by the exciting program being developed at a wide range of institutions. Some labs encourage critical and quantitative thinking, some emphasize demonstration of principles or development of lab techniques, and some help students deepen their understanding of fundamental concepts.

Where possible, the lab should be coincident with the lecture or discussion. Before you begin to develop a laboratory program, it is important to think about its goals. Here are a number of possibilities:

- Develop intuition and deepen understanding of concepts.
- Apply concepts learned in class to new situations.
- Experience basic phenomena.
- Develop critical, quantitative thinking.
- Develop experimental and data analysis skills.

- Learn to use scientific apparatus.
- Learn to estimate statistical errors and recognize systematic errors.
- Develop reporting skills (written and oral).
- Practice collaborative problem solving.
- Exercise curiosity and creativity by designing a procedure to test a hypothesis.
- Better appreciate the role of experimentation in science.
- Test important laws and rules.

Developing an effective laboratory requires appropriate space and equipment and extraordinary effort from the department's most creative teachers. Still, those who have invested in innovative introductory laboratory programs report very encouraging results: better understanding of the material, much more positive student attitudes toward the lab, and more faculty participation in the lab. Many science departments have implemented innovative laboratory programs in their introductory courses. Education sessions at professional society meetings are another opportunity to get good ideas for labs in your discipline. Some faculty members have given up lecturing and large class meetings in favor of supervised collaborative learning in laboratory settings. Such workshop methods have been devised for teaching physics, chemistry, and mathematics. Although this is not feasible at many institutions, some of the ideas developed in these courses translate reasonably well to courses in which a lab is associated with a large-enrollment course.

Students in two laboratory sections of a chemistry course for non-science majors worked in groups of three on two experiments about acids, bases, and buffers. The experiments were devised using a modified "jigsaw" technique, in which each student in a group is assigned a particular part of a lesson or unit and is responsible for helping the other members of the group learn that material. The week prior to the laboratory, students were given lists of objectives and preparatory work that were divided into three parts. Students decided how to divide the responsibility for the preparatory and laboratory tasks, but were informed that the scores from their post-laboratory exams would be averaged, and that all members of a group would receive the same grade. Two control sections of the same laboratory were conducted in a traditional manner, with students working independently. All four groups of students were part of the same lecture class, and there were no significant differences in age, gender balance, or previous number of chemistry classes. Although the control sections had an overall GPA higher than the cooperative learning sections (2.77 versus 2.30), the students in the cooperative sections had higher overall scores on the post-lab tests. The authors conclude that use of cooperative learning in the laboratory has a positive effect on student achievement. Laboratory teaching methods vary widely, but there is certainly no substitute for an instructor circulating among the students, answering and asking questions, pointing out subtle details or possible applications, and generally guiding students' learning.

Although students work informally in pairs or groups in many labs, some faculty have formally introduced cooperative learning into their labs. Some instructors rely on a lab handout, not to give cookbook instructions, but to pose a carefully constructed sequence of questions to help students design experiments which illustrate important concepts. One advantage of the well-designed handout is that the designer more closely controls what students do in the lab. The challenge is to design it so that students must think and be creative. In more unstructured labs the challenge is to prevent students from getting stranded and discouraged.

Easy access to a faculty member or teaching assistant is essential in this type of lab. Once you have decided on the goals for your laboratory, and are familiar with some of the innovative ideas in your field, you are ready to ask yourself the following questions:

- How have others operated their programs? Seek out colleagues in other departments or institutions who may have implemented a laboratory program similar to the one you are considering, and learn from their experiences.
- How much time and energy are you willing to invest? Buying new equipment and tinkering with the lab write-ups will probably improve the labs, but much more is required to implement substantial change. Changing the way that students learn involves rethinking the way the lab is taught, writing new lab handouts, setting up a training program for teaching assistants, and perhaps designing some new experiments.
- What support will you have? Solicit the interest and support of departmental colleagues and teaching assistants.
- Are the departmental and institutional administrations supportive of your project and willing to accept the risks? Determine how likely they are to provide the needed resources.
- Are you prepared to go through all of this and still get mediocre student evaluations?

Teachers discuss usual student questions and misconceptions and ideas for directing student learning. Teachers review procedures for circulating among student groups to ensure that each group gets attention. Groups are visited early to help them get started. Each group is visited several other times, but at least midway through the lab to discuss preliminary results and interpretations and toward the end of the lab to review outcomes and interpretations.

Teachers review the students' notebooks or reports and then meet to discuss difficulties and misconceptions. Discussions of grading and comments that might be made are important because these procedures can influence student performance and attitudes on subsequent exercises. The various methods by which students report their lab work have different pedagogical objectives. The formal written report teaches students how to communicate their work in journal style, but students sometimes sacrifice content for appearance. Keeping a lab notebook, which is graded, teaches the student to keep a record while doing an experiment, but it may not develop good writing and presentation skills.

Oral reports motivate students to understand their work well enough to explain it to others, but this takes time and does not give students practice in writing. Oral reports can also motivate students to keep a good notebook, especially if they can consult it during their presentation. In choosing this important aspect of the students' lab experience, consider how your students might report their work in the future.Many benefits of carefully planned laboratory exercises are realized only if the instructional staff is well prepared to teach. Often the primary, or only, lab instruction comes from graduate or undergraduate teaching assistants or from faculty members who were not involved in designing the lab. Time must be invested in training the teaching staff, focusing first on their mastery of the lab experiments and then on the method of instruction. It is a fine art to guide students without either simply giving the answer or seeming to be obstinately obscure. Teaching assistants who were not taught in this way can have difficulty adapting to innovative laboratory programs, and the suggestions below will you help you guide their transition. A good part of the success of a course depends on the group spirit of the whole team of instructor and teaching assistants. Many such groups meet weekly, perhaps in an informal but structured way, so that the teaching assistants can provide feedback to the instructor as well as learn about the most effective way to teach the next laboratory experiment.

The responsibility for preparing teaching assistants is largely dependent on the setting. While many faculty members at four-year institutions are responsible for preparing their teaching assistants, this task is handled on a department-wide or campus-wide basis in programs with large numbers of graduate students. Some even have argued that one of the main causes of the crisis in science education is the failure of colleges and universities to do an adequate job of preparing future science teachers. The heart of the matter is this: improving undergraduate science education has a direct, positive effect on precollege education. An undergraduate science teacher who models real scientific skills of investigation and critical thinking, and applies those skills to new situations, can make an enormous contribution to the education of those students who will not only use the model, but eventually will teach it. Most teachers of undergraduates have students in their classes who will need to share scientific understanding and skills with others, perhaps as a trial lawyer or a track coach, or as a member of a citizen's action group.

Some of your students will likely become science teachers at the elementary level and have the opportunity to intro duce curious children to important scientific concepts. Others may become secondary science teachers with responsibility for teaching advanced courses for college-bound students. Those who have studied science teaching are divided over how best to teach future science teachers. Some argue that future teachers need distinctly different instruction that is more hands-on, active, and problem oriented than what a future scientist might need. Others argue that future teachers need the same type of instruction as scientists; in other words, the future teacher should be treated like a future scientist while learning.

2

Role of ICTs in Curriculum Development

Information and communication technology (ICT) offers new and exciting possibilities for enhancing the way we work and play. Many people, regardless of skill level, experience a high level of stress associated with using technologies of all kinds. Organisations that have adopted technical approaches to the use of technology are finding that their employees are more than a little 'teched-off' with the technology over people approach. Makers of communication products understand the importance of developing interesting and creative applications that fit people's lifestyles.

Schools face challenges to find creative uses of technology that engage young people and make a difference in learning. Young people actively engage in rich and complex technological contexts that contrast sharply with their school experience that they often find irrelevant and frustrating. For many teachers their experience of new technologies is limited and they often resist its use. This situation is exasperated by the fact that educational systems all around the world now link educational reform with the creative and reflective applications of technology.

Adopting more reflective approaches to technological use can help us 'look behind' the application to focus more on the educational benefits. Reflective approaches also require recognition of the inherent tension in the technological proposition. Technology can be used to strengthen communities and give voice to individuals and groups previously silenced, or it can become a tool of control serving the interests of governments and/or multinational capitalism. Both views are current and compete for expression just as alternate views for schooling—to free individuals or to prepare them for citisenship—compete in the development of the school curriculum.

As educators engage with these different views, they will find themselves involved in the dialogue between these opposing schools of thought. For example, on the one hand, educational publishers and other commercial interests are looking seriously at ICT as a way of delivering goods and services into schools while on the other hand, communities explore ways of using it as a means of collaboration and resource sharing. Facing the challenges of using ICT in educationally productive ways requires a rethinking of the place of ICT in education and a consideration of the ways to promote the development of creative contexts for thinking and learning.

There is a growing band of commentators that present compelling cases for re-thinking how we have used technology in schools to date. A common theme emerging from these views is the need to reconsider not just the how but also the why of ICT use. Cuban questions the claimed benefits of technology and has called for the proponents to examine their assumptions and work to develop a broader vision of the contribution of ICT to education. A proponent of technology, Becker in many ways agrees that technology has not transformed teaching and learning, however he argues that many of the problems arise from the narrow and technical focus of the educational applications. He concludes that in situations where teachers and students engage in authentic and deep learning there are more encouraging outcomes.

Numerous critics argue that many uses of technology represent a failure to engage with students and their experience. Some go as far as to suggest that these effects are potentially damaging. Even without needing to accept the fundamental premises of these critics' views, there is a strong imperative to re-consider the use of ICT. In today's social and political climate, the focus on the economic costs of ICT is also important. In a recent review of ICT research, Angrist and Lavy conclude that "the costs are clear-cut the benefits are murky." The challenges for research and evaluation in this area are highlighted by Rowe who suggests that ICT must be seen as more than a narrow technical experimental treatment or effect.

Postman makes an important distinction between views of technology as 'additive' as opposed to 'evolutionary'. He argues that technology transforms the social landscape and thus any evaluation or critique must acknowledge the changed social context. The creative application of ICT changes the context of teaching and learning and "alters the collaborative interaction and shared dialogue between students and teachers". Research and evaluation must adopt more multidimensional approaches to monitor both the changes that take place in the cultures of classrooms/ schools and the changes in students. At present, most measures of ICT learning seem to focus more on skills than knowledge creation.

The term information age" no longer adequately describes the era in which we live. Instead, the knowledge age or network economy" means that the valued commodity is no longer routine and disembodied information, but rather the processes humans use to work together to create new knowledge and innovate. In this new era, views of human knowledge and development that do not acknowledge the interaction of context are inadequate. Increasingly, educational policy is also recognising that an emphasis on mass knowledge and its transmission is only partially useful, and that there is also a need to understand the social and cultural base of knowledge development and human action.

However, the extent to which educational practice haskept pace with these developments is still somewhatlimited. In The Children's Machine: Rethinking Schoolin the Age of the Computer, Seymour Papert posed a thought experiment in which a group of timetravellers from the past, comprising a group of surgeonsand a group of school teachers, visit their modern-dayworkplaces. The surgeons find the developments inmedical knowledge and the application of newtechnologies have transformed practice while theteachers notice few changes.In a recent review of the theories that underpinrecent ICT applications, Merrill concluded thatmany of these theories share similar learning principlesthat are representative of what has been seen as thebroader philosophical shift from instructionist toconstructivist accounts of learning. While constructivism provides rich accounts of learning, there is limited discussion or reconciliation of the relationship between individual and social learning.

There is evidence pointing to the benefits of adopting constructivist-type approaches to the integration of information technology into teaching and learning. There is also evidence that "instructionist" approaches often increase a teacher 's reluctance to adopt new technologies. The role of teacher education is to develop both technosavvy and child-centred teachers. Clearly there is a greater need to develop a more integrated focus on teaching and learning with ICT as both a context for learning and a set of practical skills. At the school level, effective technology integration also requires systemic institutional reform that must be supported by appropriate leadership.

In schools, the form ICT will take and the functions it will serve for teaching and learning will be determined largely by the framework and perspectives that school communities choose to adopt. School communities must ask themselves: Does their use of ICT simply serve curriculum as another resource or does it transform what it means to be a learner in the knowledge age? Does it strengthen local communities or serve other interests? Does it position students as consumers of information or as creators of knowledge? Experience arising from working with teachers shows that answers to these and other important questions are most often realized when school communities engage with ICT on a more regular and confident basis. However, it is equally important that schools develop a critical view of what might be possible now and in the future. As learning organisations schools cannot ignore these questions.

As dialogue is a key characteristic of any learning organisation this must be enabled in such a way to allow all stakeholders, individually and collectively, to work to produce results that matter. Quite clearly, the use of ICT in education is no longer simply a teacher or student issue—it is a school development issue. In order to do this we need to develop a broader understanding of ICT and initiate a sustained dialogue grounded in pedagogical frameworks within which ICT is no longer seen as a technical issue but rather a whole school challenge that is focused on improving learning outcomes for children.

Creative Learning Contexts

Cultural-historical activity theory sees the development of thinking processes and human activity as intimately related. This more systemic view argues that successful technological innovation requires a deep understanding of its social and cultural setting. One implication arising from this view is that many educational innovations are often stifled by contextual factors. With respect to ICT innovation these factors can take the many forms such as exam-oriented pedagogy, unsupportive leadership, resistant teachers, irrelevant learning tasks all the way through to problems of fragmented timetabling and classroom layout.Experienced educators understand the powerful influence of these factors.

In the area of psychology, Quarts & Sejnowski argue that traditional views of intelligence have been the biggest obstacle to creating smart cultures. In education, teacher-centred and exam-oriented approaches to education and schooling often stifle individual creatively and hinder educational innovation. There is also evidence from brain science that this can impact on brain development. The brain's capacity to change its structure and function is known as plasticity. The brain has evolved with a capacity for life-long learning developed in response to being immersed in a complex and changing world. Animal studies reveal that the most significant brain changes occur when the animal's environment is regularly changed. The key implication is that our brains need stimulation and novelty. Routine and highly structured environments do not offer these opportunities.

There is promising work that is showing how teaching programmes can be developed to build and strengthen an individual brain function. Psychology (and education) used to hold individual differences up as the main source of variation in performance. It is quite likely that the availability and use of technological tools in creative contexts will be a new source of variance offering a very real opportunity to leverage individual differences in highly productive ways.

A focus on the use of ICT as knowledge creation is also dependent on the design of contexts or spaces for thinking and learning. Vygotsky and Luria argued that tool-use shapes and re-shapes thinking processes. As context changes, those thinking processes also change. They are not fixed and unchanging but rather plastic and formed by practical activity. Many current uses of ICT in schools are skillsbased and characterised by set routines and fixed instructional sequences and activities. Many of these uses require little creativity on the part of students and thus have limited impact on thinking processes. Though these are an important form of thinking, it is quite clear that the next generation of thinkers must develop more relational and reflective forms of thinking. It follows that our goal should be about designing activities and contexts for learning that both generates new knowledge and provides-contexts that shape more creative and reflective forms of thinking.

The concepts of multiliteracies and technoliteracies work against a view of technology from a technical perspective. In these views, integrating ICT into school curriculum without examining the pedagogical implications of practice fails to engage with the realities of today's changing world—a world of rapid technological and economic change that requires flexible and strong problem-solvers. In this regard ICT is seen both as a form of information literacy dealing with the effective use of technologies, and the basis for the development of higher-order thinking and problemsolving.

Information literacy is a dialogic process that is fundamentally active and communicative rather than passive and informational. The main point to take from these views is the importance of seeing the design of ICT-based activities as an open-ended and collaborative process. While there are useful examples of using ICT to promote higher-level thinking, for project-based learning and Webquests, all of these approaches still draw largely on instructionist models and there is still a need for broader collaborative knowledge creation approaches.

The continuing challenge to integrating ICT effectively is that of moving away from narrow and technical views of technology in teaching and learning. The idea of smart and more integrated uses of technologies is supported by studies of successful business organisations. In his book *Good-to-Great,* Jim Collins shows how effective businesses work hard to create a will or momentum for growth and then choose appropriate technologies to accelerate that growth. The impetus for change and growth is based around the core business goals and not solely the desire for change or technology-use per se. Successful organisations think differently about technology and respond to the pressure of change with thoughtfulness, creativity and design.

An example of a collaborative approach to knowledge creation can be seen in recent work that is promoting a new model of design through the development of collaborative knowledge creation tools. Based on software known as group decision support systems (GDSS), these tools were originally developed in Australia to support decision making in business settings and in recent years have been adapted to facilitate collaborative learning.

The team learning systems (TLS) in its most recent implementation has features that record and document the expertise of people skilled in human interaction and knowledge formation. In many implementations, this expertise is presented as pre-structured open-ended questions to a group in either a face-to-face or distributed setting. In its room-based form, twelve keyboards are connected via a multiplexer to a computer, allowing everyone to "talk" at the same time and view the ideas as they are being created or further manipulated. A real context or question is posed and the participants follow different design-etiquettes to solve problems and produce knowledge outcomes.

The system allows participants to operate both as individuals and as part of a team in a variety of contexts. Concept development takes place more intuitively, in a manner more like the way "private thoughts" evolve, as opposed to the more formal and structured way of taking turns to present opinions and positions. The TLS also has voting tools that allow participants to respond simultaneously in public or private to propositions, either as a single question or sequence of questions, and then tabulate and chart the group inputs.

The tools comprise a Yes-No vote, Multiple Choice, Weight, Rank, XY, Scale, and Team Questionnaire. The success of these types of tools appears to be due largely to the way that students are given access to high level cognitive expertise allowing them to co-create new knowledge. The knowledge creation process is highly collaborative and open-ended but still involves design and facilitation.

Activities for Teaching

The actual play occurs when science teachers act on the basic content and well-reasoned arguments for inclusion of evolution and the nature of science in school science programmes. Following are the activities for teaching about evolution and the nature of science:

Introducing Inquiry and the Nature of Science

This activity introduces basic procedures involved in inquiry and concepts describing the nature of science. In the first portion of the activity the teacher uses a numbered cube to involve students in asking a question—what is on the bottom?— and the students propose an explanation based on their observations. Then the teacher presents the students with a second cube and asks them to use the available evidence to propose an explanation for what is on the bottom of this cube. Finally, students design a cube that they exchange and use for an evaluation. This activity provides students with opportunities to learn the abilities and understandings aligned with science as inquiry and the nature of science as described in the National Science Education Standards.

Designed for grades 5 through 12, the activity requires a total of four class periods to complete. Lower grade levels might only complete the first cube and the evaluation where students design a problem based on the cube activity. This activity provides all students with opportunities to develop abilities of scientific inquiry as described in the National Science Education Standards. Specifically, it enables them to:

- identify questions that can be answered through scientific investigations,

- design and conduct a scientific investigation,
- use appropriate tools and techniques to gather, analyse, and interpret data,
- develop descriptions, explanations, predictions, and models using evidence,
- think critically and logically to make relationships between evidence and explanations,
- recognise and analyse alternative explanations and predictions, and
- communicate scientific procedures and explanations.

This activity also provides all students opportunities to develop understanding about inquiry and the nature of science as described in the National Science Education Standards. Specifically, it introduces the following concepts:

- Different kinds of questions suggest different kinds of scientific investigations.
- Current scientific knowledge and understanding guide scientific investigations.
- Technology used to gather data enhances accuracy and allows scientists to analyse and quantify results of investigations.
- Scientific explanations emphasise evidence, have logically consistent arguments, and use scientific principles, models, and theories.
- Science distinguishes itself from other ways of knowing and from other bodies of knowledge through the use of empirical standards, logical arguments, and skepticism, as scientists strive for the best possible explanations about the natural world.

The pursuit of scientific explanations often begins with a question about a natural phenomenon. Science is a way of developing answers, or improving explanations, for observations or events in the natural world. The scientific question can emerge from a child's curiosity about where the dinosaurs went or why the sky is blue. Or the question can extend scientists' inquiries into the process of extinction or the chemistry of ozone depletion. Once the question is asked, a process of scientific inquiry begins, and there eventually may be an answer or a proposed explanation.

Critical aspects of science include curiosity and the freedom to pursue that curiosity. Other attitudes and habits of mind that characterise scientific inquiry and the activities of scientists include intelligence, honesty, skepticism, tolerance for ambiguity, openness to new knowledge, and the willingness to share knowledge publicly. Scientific inquiry includes systematic approaches to observing, collecting information, identifying significant variables, formulating and testing hypotheses, and taking precise, accurate, and reliable measurements.

Understanding and designing experiments are also part of the inquiry process. Scientific explanations are more than the results of collecting and organising data. Scientists also engage in important processes such as constructing laws, elaborating models, and developing hypotheses based on data. These processes extend, clarify, and unite the observations and data and, very importantly, develop deeper and broader explanations. Examples include the taxonomy of organisms, the periodic table of the elements, and theories of common descent and natural selection. One characteristic of science is that many explanations continually change. Two types of changes occur in scientific explanations: new explanations are developed, and old explanations are modified.

Just because someone asks a question about an object, organism, or event in nature does not necessarily mean that person is pursuing a scientific explanation. Among the conditions that must be met to make explanations scientific are the following:

- Scientific explanations are based on empirical observations or experiments. The appeal to authority as a valid explanation does not meet the requirements of science. Observations are based on sense experiences or on an extension of the senses through technology.
- Scientific explanations are made public. Scientists make presentations at scientific meetings or publish in professional journals, making knowledge public and available to other scientists.
- Scientific explanations are tentative. Explanations can and do change. There are no scientific truths in an absolute sense.
- Scientific explanations are historical. Past explanations are the basis for contemporary explanations, and those, in turn, are the basis for future explanations.
- Scientific explanations are probabilistic. The statistical view of nature is evident implicitly or explicitly when stating scientific predictions of phenomena or explaining the likelihood of events in actual situations.
- Scientific explanations assume cause-effect relationships. Much of science is directed toward determining causal relationships and developing explanations for interactions and linkages between objects, organisms, and events. Distinctions among causality, correlation, coincidence, and contingency separate science from pseudoscience.

- Scientific explanations are limited. Scientific explanations sometimes are limited by technology, for example, the resolving power of microscopes and telescopes. New technologies can result in new fields of inquiry or extend current areas of study. The interactions between technology and advances in molecular biology and the role of technology in planetary explorations serve as examples.
- Science cannot answer all questions. Some questions are simply beyond the parameters of science. Many questions involving the meaning of life, ethics, and theology are examples of questions that science cannot answer.

The Formulation of Explanatons: An invitation to inquiry on natural selection

This activity uses the concept of natural selection to introduce the idea of formulating and testing scientific hypotheses. Through a focused discussion approach, the teacher provides information and allows students time to think, interact with peers, and propose explanations for observations described by the teacher. The teacher then provides more information, and the students continue their discussion based on the new information. This activity will help students in grades 5 through 8 develop several abilities related to scientific inquiry and formulate understandings about the nature of science as presented in the National Science Education Standards. This activity provides all students with opportunities to develop the abilities of scientific inquiry as described in the National Science Education Standards. Specifically, it enables them to:

- identify questions that can be answered through scientific investigations,

- design and conduct a scientific investigation,
- use appropriate tools and techniques to gather, analyse, and interpret data,
- develop descriptions, explanations, predictions, and models using evidence,
- think critically and logically to make relationships between evidence and explanations,
- recognise and analyse alternative explanations and predictions, and
- communicate scientific procedures and explanations.

This activity also provides all students opportunities to develop understandings about inquiry, the nature of science, and biological evolution as described in the National Science Education Standards. Specifically, it conveys the following concepts:

- Different kinds of questions suggest different kinds of scientific investigations.
- Current scientific knowledge and understanding guide scientific investigations.
- Technology used to gather data enhances accuracy and allows scientists to analyse and quantify results of investigations.
- Scientific explanations emphasise evidence, have logically consistent arguments, and use scientific principles, models, and theories.
- Species evolve over time. Evolution is the consequence of the interactions of (1) the potential for a species to increase its numbers, (2) the genetic variability of offspring due to mutation and recombination of genes, (3) a finite supply of the resources required for life, and

(4) the ensuing selection of those offspring better able to survive and leave offspring in a particular environment.

Many biological theories can be thought of as developing in five interrelated and overlapping stages. The first is a period of extensive observation of nature or analysing the results of experiments. Darwin's observations would be an example of the former. Second, these observations lead scientists to ponder questions of "how" and "why." In the course of answering these questions, scientists infer explanations or make conjectures as working hypotheses. Third, in most cases, scientists submit hypotheses to formal, rigorous tests to check the validity of the hypotheses. At this point the hypotheses can be confirmed, falsified and rejected (not supported with evidence), or modified based on the evidence.

Investigating Natural Selection

In this activity, the students experience one mechanism for evolution through a simulation that models the principles of natural selection and helps answer the question: How might biological change have occurred and been reinforced over time? The activity is designed for grades 9 through 12 and requires three class periods. This activity provides all students opportunities to develop understandings of biological evolution as described in the National Science Education Standards. Specifically, it conveys the concepts that: Species evolve over time.

Evolution is the consequence of the interaction of

(1) the potential for a species to increase in number,

(2) the genetic variability of offspring due to mutation and recombination of genes,

(3) a finite supply of the resources required for life, and

(4) the ensuing selection of those offspring better able to survive and leave offspring in a particular environment. Item 4 is the primary emphasis of this activity. Teachers can introduce the other factors as appropriate.

Natural selection and its evolutionary consequences provide a scientific explanation for the fossil record of ancient life forms, as well as for the striking molecular similarities observed among the diverse species of living organisms. Some living organisms have the capacity to produce populations of almost infinite size, but environments and resources are finite. The fundamental tension has profound effects on the interactions among organisms. Many students have difficulty with the fundamental concepts of evolution. For example, some students express misconceptions about natural selection because they do not understand the relationship between variations within a population and the potential effect of those variations as the population continues to grow in numbers in an environment with limited resources. This is a dynamic understanding that derives from the four ideas presented in the learning outcomes for this activity. This activity emphasises natural selection.

In particular, it presents students with the predator-prey relationship as one example of how natural selection operates in nature. Students should understand that the process of evolution has two steps, referred to as genetic variation and natural selection. The first step is the development of genetic variation through changes such as genetic recombination, gene flow, and mutations. The second step, and the point of this activity, is selection. Differential survival and reproduction of organisms is due to a variety of environmental factors such as predator-prey relationships, resource shortages, and change of habitat. In any generation only a small percentage of organisms survives. Survival depends on an organism's genetic constitution that will, given circumstances such as limited resources, give a greater probability of survival and reproduction.

Investigating Common Descent: Formulating Explanations and Models

In this activity, students formulate explanations and models that simulate structural and biochemical data as they investigate the misconception that humans evolved from apes. The activities require two 45-minute periods. This activity provides opportunities for all students to develop abilities of scientific inquiry as described in the National Science Education Standards. Specifically, it enables them to:

- formulate descriptions, explanations, predictions, and models using evidence,
- think critically and logically to make relationships between evidence and explanations, and
- recognise and analyse alternative explanations and predictions.

In addition, the activity provides all students opportunities to develop fundamental understandings in the life sciences as described in the US' National Science Education Standards. Specifically, it conveys the following concepts:

- In all organisms, the instructions for specifying the characteristics of the organism are carried in DNA, a large polymer formed from subunits of four kinds (A, G, C, and T). The chemical and structural properties of DNA explain how the genetic information that underlies heredity is both encoded in genes and replicated (by a templating mechanism).

- The millions of different species of plants, animals, and microorganisms that live on earth today are related by descent from common ancestors.
- Biological classifications are based on how organisms are related. Organisms are classified into a hierarchy of groups and subgroups based on similarities that reflect their evolutionary relationships. The species is the most fundamental unit of classification.

Proposing Explanations for Fossil Footprints

In this activity, students observe and interpret "fossil footprint" evidence. From the evidence, they are asked to construct defensible hypotheses or explanations for events that took place in the geological past. The estimated time requirement for this activity is two class periods. This activity is designed for grades 5 through 8. This activity provides all students an opportunity to develop the abilities of scientific inquiry and understanding of the nature of science. Specifically, it enables them to:

- propose explanations and make predictions based on evidence,
- recognise and analyse alternative explanations and predictions,
- understand that scientific explanations are subject to change as new evidence becomes available,
- understand that scientific explanations must meet certain criteria.

First and foremost, they must be consistent with experimental and observational evidence about nature, and must make accurate predictions, when appropriate, about systems being studied. They should also be logical, respect the rules of evidence, be open to criticism, report methods and procedures, and make knowledge public. Explanations of how the natural world changes based on myths, personal beliefs, religious values, mystical inspiration, superstition, or authority may be personally useful and socially relevant, but they are not scientific. This activity provides teachers with the opportunity to help students realise the differences between observations and inferences. In terms of the Standards, it centers on the development of explanations based on evidence. It encourages students to think critically about the inferences they make and about the logical relationships between cause and effect.

Understanding Earth's Changes Over Time

Comparing the magnitude of geologic time with spans of time in a person's lifetime is difficult for many students. In this activity, students use a long paper strip and a reasonable scale to represent visually all of geologic time, including significant events in the development of life on earth as well as recent human events. This activity provides all students with an opportunity to develop understandings of the earth systems. Specifically, it introduces them to the following concepts:

- A mathematical scale representing the length of geologic time.
- The relationship of time between human events, events in earth's history, and the total age of the earth.
- The formation of the sun, the earth, and the rest of the solar system from a nebular cloud of dust and gas 4.6 billion years ago.

- The estimation of geologic time by observing rock sequences and using fossils to correlate the sequences at various locations. A current method of dating earth materials uses the known decay rates of radioactive isotopes present in rocks to measure the time since the rock was formed.
- The ongoing evolution of the earth system resulting from interactions among the solid earth, the oceans, the atmosphere, and organisms.
- The evidence for one-celled forms of life—the bacteria—extending back more than 3.5 billion years. The evolution of life caused dramatic changes in the composition of the earth's atmosphere, which did not originally contain oxygen.

Proposing the Theory of Biological Evolution: Historical Perspective

This activity uses evolution to introduce students to historical perspectives and the nature of science. The teacher has students read short excerpts of original statements on evolution from Jean Lamarck, Charles Darwin, and Alfred Russel Wallace. This activity is intended as either a supplement to other investigations or as a core activity. The activity provides all students with opportunities to develop understandings of the history and nature of science as described in the National Science Education Standards. Specifically, it conveys the following concepts:

- Scientists are influenced by societal, cultural, and personal beliefs and ways of viewing the world. Science is not separate from society but rather a part of society.
- Scientific explanations must meet certain criteria. First and foremost, they must be consistent with

experimental and observational evidence about nature, and they must make accurate predictions, when appropriate, about the systems being studied. They should also be logical, respect the rules of evidence, be open to criticism, report methods and procedures, and make knowledge public. Explanations of how the natural world changes based on myths, personal beliefs, religious values, mystical inspiration, superstition, or authority may be personally useful and socially relevant, but they are not scientific.

Because all scientific ideas depend on experimental and observational confirmation, all scientific knowledge is in principle subject to change as new evidence becomes available. The core ideas of science, such as the conservation of energy or the laws of motion, have been subjected to a wide variety of confirmations and are therefore unlikely to change in the areas in which they have been tested. In areas where data or understanding are incomplete, such as the details of human evolution or questions surrounding global warming, new data may well lead to changes in current ideas or resolve current conflicts.

In situations where information is still fragmentary, it is normal for scientific ideas to be incomplete, but this is also where the opportunity for making advances may be greatest. Occasionally, there are advances in science and technology that have important and long-lasting effects on science and society. The historical perspective of scientific explanations demonstrates how scientific knowledge changes by evolving over time, almost always building on earlier knowledge.

Connecting Population Growth and Biological Evolution

In this activity, students develop a model of the

mathematical nature of population growth. The investigation provides an excellent opportunity for consideration of the population growth of plant and animal species and the resultant stresses that contribute to natural selection. The activity is based on an original activity from the Earth Science Curriculum Project. It is used with permission. This activity provides all students an opportunity to develop understandings about scientific inquiry and biological evolution as described in the National Science Education Standards. Specifically, it conveys the following concepts:

- Mathematics is essential in scientific inquiry. Mathematical tools and models guide and improve the posing of questions, gathering data, constructing explanations, and communicating results.
- Species evolve over time. Evolution is the consequence of (1) the potential for a species to increase its numbers, (2) the genetic variability of offspring due to mutation and recombination of genes, (3) a finite supply of the resources required for life, and (4) the ensuing selection of those offspring better able to survive and leave offspring in a particular environment. (Item 1 is the primary content emphasis of this activity. Teachers can introduce the other factors as appropriate.)
- Populations grow or decline through the combined effects of births and deaths and through emigration and immigration into specific areas. Populations can increase through linear or exponential growth, with effects on resource use and on environmental pollution.
- Populations can reach limits to growth. Carrying capacity is the maximum number of organisms that can be supported by a given environment.

- Living organisms have the capacity to produce populations of arbitrarily large size, but environments and resources are finite. This fundamental tension has profound effects on the interactions between organisms.

3

Teaching of Communication Skills

Cognitive Processing

Cognitive processing of the information probably begins prior to the actual lecture, as students set up and prepare to take notes. In most cases, they have already begun thinking about the topic. In other words, for some students the topic itself stimulates thoughts and memories about it. For example, if the topic is "frogs," many students have already begun recalling thoughts from long-term memory about their experiences, good and bad, with frogs. Whether they are thinking about the frog they caught at camp or the frog they recently dissected in science class, their thoughts are already on today's topic and now these memories will help serve to personalise or flavour their notes for the day.

But, this only the start of processing information about that particular day's lecture topic. Cognitive processing also involves distinguishing between essential lecture information and nonessential information, determining foreign terms or unknown vocabulary, storing bits of lecture information in short-term memory long enough to accurately record it, and paraphrasing and elaborating on lecture points. For many students, difficulty with any of these tasks, may use up precious reserves in short-term memory resulting in fewer lecture points recorded or less complete lecture points recorded. The ability to pick and choose only the important main ideas from the lecturer, and then supplement the ideas with details, appears to be one key to processing notes efficiently.

Notes Writing and Recording

Finally, as students process the information, they must also accurately record lecture points. Writing down or recording notes involves writing information down in a succinct yet usable format. Too sparse notes and the information may not be understandable later: too much detail in notes and the student may miss other relevant lecture points because they are too busy recording previous lecture information. The key seems to be recording important lecture points at a reasonably fast rate to keep up with the lecturer. As students record notes, using shorthand or abbreviations appears to be a real plus to recording notes efficiently, as does the ability to record lecture information in an organised manner.

Reviewing Notes

In addition to listening, writing and processing skills, the ability to review notes is also an important, yet overlooked step in note-taking. Whether it be a review of notes immediately after class, or studying notes for a test, the review process is an important one. Here too, the task of reviewing notes can have potential pitfalls for students. Reviewing notes often means looking over notes immediately after class to fill in gaps, clarify poorly understood concepts, or correcting the spelling and legibility of handwriting. For many students, reviewing notes is often the step missing from their note-taking repertoire of skills. Yet, this step could allow poor note-takers to compensate for note-taking inadequacies. The key during this step is to review notes immediately after class. In this way, the topic is still fresh in mind and it becomes part of a routine for students.

MULTITASKING

There appear to be four keys to multitasking during note-taking. During the listening stage, focusing attention to the topic and lecture is important. Students should not only be prepared to take notes, but maintain attention throughout the lecture. During the cognitive process stage, students must choose relevant lecture points and then add details to personalise the content. Being able to "read" the instructor's cues is crucial step for determining important lecture points. These cues may vary from teacher to teacher and may be the reason why some students take better notes in certain classes. During recording of notes, the student should be able to write the relevant lecture points at a sufficiently fast pace and in an organised manner.

Of course, if the information is presented in an organised manner to begin with, students then can simply record the notes in a chronological or hierarchical manner. Finally, immediately after the lecture, students should review their notes for gaps or areas of misunderstanding. If teachers can allot five minutes for this prior to class ending, this task could become part of a daily routine.

Learning Opportunities in Taking Notes

Because taking notes presents two opportunities to learn the information (i.e., once in class and later as they review their notes or study their notes for a test), teachers should try to maximise these opportunities for students. The more that teachers can do to present the crucial information (i.e., those important lecture points) in a clearly organised manner, the easier it will be for students to understand the content and record notes. During the listening phase, teachers should present lecture information so that it gets students' attention.

Anything that the teacher can do to draw attention to the important aspects of the lecture will help students record more notes. For example, simply writing important lecture points on the board can increase the likelihood that the same information will be found in students' notes. Calling attention to notes through "verbal signposts" or "lecture cues" has also been shown to result in a greater number of notes recorded by students. Signposts are those statements used to alert students to important lecture points. For example, "an important point to remember is" or "there are six parts to a cell." Signposts such as these have purported to result in students recording a greater number of notes and higher achievement.

Pausing or changing verbal intonation can also signal to students that an important lecture point is about to be presented. Typically, the lecturer's pause indicates to students that they should be writing down information. In terms of helping students write faster, teachers can use abbreviations and teach students shorthand (i.e., "how" to abbreviate). Any of these techniques will help students to record more notes. Slowing down the rate of the lecture is also another technique that can aid students in recording more notes. Placing pauses in lectures allows them to catch up with the lecture.

Some researchers have conducted studies in which the instructor alternated sections of their lecture between listening and note-taking. During the note-taking sections students recorded notes and during other sections students simply listened to the lecture. Both methods can reduce the pace of a lecture and, in the process, allow students to take more and higher quality notes. Finally, reviewing notes serves to assist students in filling in gaps and aiding understanding of information. Using designated pauses during the lecture, such as the pause procedure, allows students to review their notes with another student.

Typically, students are paired together and at natural breaks in the lecture, students are given a two-minute break to discuss their notes with a partner. Using the pause procedure in which students reviewed notes, studies have shown that students were able increase their recall and comprehension of lecture information. Reviewing notes immediately after recording them has also been shown to be effective at increasing comprehension of lecture information. For example, Lazarus used a review period following student use of guided notes. This condition produced the greatest gains on measures of comprehension of the lecture. Despite the type of procedure used, research has shown that reviewing notes results in greater gains.

Tips for a Better Note-taker

Application Activities: If the information is really important, teachers will give an activity that applies the information that they just presented. If teachers give you an activity, go back to your notes and place a big star next to that lecture information.

Lecture Cues: Right before a teacher presents important lecture points they will say something like "it is really important to remember that..." or "you should remember that...". These are called lecture cues or verbal signposts. Teachers say these statements to let students know that the information that follows is really important stuff. Again, place a big old star next to these lecture points. Of course, the obvious lecture cue is "this will be on the test."

Long Pauses: The teacher "pauses" and is silent for a minute or two after they make a statement. Usually a pause of 60 to 120 seconds means that this information is so important that the teacher will give you time to write it in your notes. Again consider placing a star next to these lecture points.

Repeating Information: Either the teacher says the information a second (or third) time or other students ask the teacher to repeat what was just said. It must be important if the teacher repeats it.

Notes on the Board (Or Overhead): If the teacher writes or spells words, write them down along with detailed information about the words. Usually, a teacher will spell new vocabulary or really important words. If the teacher places notes on the board, they should be in your notebook.

Speaks Louder or Slower: If the teacher speaks loader or slows down their presentation, it usually means they want you to write down the information that was just presented. Again, if they slow down their presentation, consider starring the information.

Disorganised Behaviour

The biggest challenge many students face is not learning to read or mastering the multiplication tables but rather getting organised. They may have good reasoning ability and well-developed academic skills, but they get failing grades when it comes to the nuts and bolts of learning-bringing the proper materials to class, keeping track of papers, using time wisely, writing down assignments correctly, turning them in on time. Such a seemingly simple task as bringing a pencil to class may elude the disorganised student.

The lack of these school survival skills may affect almost every phase of his school performance as well as frustrate his teacher, who may need to spend considerable class time keeping him on track. A student can lack organisational skills for a variety of reasons, including poor motivation, stress, and depression. In addition, a child with a learning or attentional disability will often exhibit this problem. Disorganised behaviour may also reflect disorganised thinking, which may manifest itself in the form of difficulty seeing patterns, organising and classifying information, and understanding sequence.

As a result, the student may have problems retrieving information, keeping track of materials, and planning things out. It is not hard to recognise a disorganised student. Displaying an almost magical ability, the disorganised student can make papers disappear in the blink of an eye. The problems of the care often most apparent in his homework habits. He may forget to write down the assignment and not remember what to do. Or he may write it down, but record it incorrectly. Or he may write it down accurately, but forget to bring the correct materials home. Or he may complete it, but forget to bring it in to school. Getting the disorganised student to develop good homework habits can exasperate the most experienced of teachers. The disorganised student may exhibit the following characteristics in your class:

- forgets to bring the proper materials
- is not ready to work when the bell rings
- is inattentive and distractible
- is often confused about what to do
- has trouble remembering information such as his school schedule
- has a messy desk and backpack
- loses papers and school materials
- turns work in late and sometimes not at all
- uses time inefficiently
- produces written work that is hard to follow
- has a problem getting started with a project or report
- has a poor sense of time
- writes down assignments inaccurately or does not write them down at all
- has difficulty expressing himself in an organised, sequential manner
- is at risk for a learning disability

The ability to be organised is one of the key building blocks of school success. It is also a skill— one that can, and should, be taught in school. You can use the following practical strategies to help your students manage their school responsibilities:

Provide Structure and Routine: Disorganised students often have trouble keeping things in order and retaining information. You can lessen their confusion by providing structure and establishing routine. Spell out the rules of your classroom clearly and simply, and tell your students what materials they must bring to class daily. Class schedules can be confusing to students, especially if they have a number of teachers or leave class for school programmes such as music lessons or speech therapy. Try to schedule activities at the same time every week. Have students with complex schedules write them out and tape them on their desks or inside their binders. Make sure they know how to read the schedule.

State Directions Clearly and Simply: Use a minimum of words to explain what the student must do. Do not give him every detail, or he will miss the key points. Also, avoid giving him multistep directions. Have him repeat your directions to ensure that he understands them. If you are explaining a complex task, demonstrate it to him, and then have him do it while you observe.

Require Students to Use a Three-Ring Binder: Consider requiring your students as early as third grade to organise their materials and schoolwork in a three-ring binder with subject dividers, blank notebook paper, and a plastic pouch for pens, pencils, and erasers. Suggest that they get a binder with pockets, one of which can be designated "To bring home" (for assignments to be completed, notes to parents, and papers to bring home and leave there) and the other "To bring to school" (for completed assignments, notes from parents, and signed parent permission slips).

Have Students Use a Container for Small Items: These items are easily lost in a desk or backpack. In trying to find a pencil, a student may create a disruption in the classroom—and a greater mess in his desk— as he rummages through his desk. Make sure your students have a case for such items as pencils, pens, erasers, and scissors. This might be a plastic zippered pouch kept in the binder or a box or resealable plastic bag kept in the desk.

Have Students Keep Their Work in Folders: Many students use the "crumple and cram" method of storing papers. To help them organise their papers so they can get them when they need them, suggest that they keep them in folders in their binders or their desks. They might have a folder for completed work, one for work to be done, and one for parent information— or they might have different colour-coded folders for each subject. Three-hole-punched folders that have pockets and fit into binders are useful ways to store papers. Help students figure out what to do with papers they no longer need. You might have them bring folders with completed work home on a specific day of the week. Let parents know when to expect the folders. After the parents review the work, their children can decide whether to store them at home or to discard them.

Present Assignments Clearly: Pay attention to how you communicate assignments to your students to ensure that they get the correct information. Be clear about the due date, the page numbers, the format, the expected length, and the required materials. Write the assignment on the board in the same place every day, and keep it posted there. If you hand out papers to be completed, include the due date on them. Ask students if they have any questions about the assignment, and give them time to write it down. Have them start difficult assignments before they leave your class, in case they have any questions. Emphasise that you expect assignments to be handed in on time. If they are not, let students know they must still complete them anyway.

Require Your Students to Write Assignments Down: Give them a choice of how— but not whether— they will do this. They might use a small assignment pad or datebook, which can be kept in the backpack or binder. A monthly assignment calendar also works well (make sure they know how to read a calendar). The calendar should be placed near the front of the binder and is most effective if it is made up of two pages that face each other, to allow more room for the recording of assignments. You might develop and hand out to your students monthly an assignment and events calendar, perhaps using a computer software programme such as Calendar Maker by Prairie Group to create it. Note birthdays, vacations, and special events on the calendar. Be sure the calendar squares are big enough to allow students to write in assignment information. Another option for recording homework is a three-hole-punched student planning book, which can be placed into a binder. Whatever system your students use, instruct them to record assignments on the due dates, and to note tests and projects. Make time to check the assignment-recording methods of your students.

Record Your Daily Assignments on a Telephone Message System for Students to Call: Talk with your principal about looking into a programme that allows you and other teachers to do this. Once it is implemented, students will not have the excuse that they did not copy down the assignment. In addition, it will allow students who are absent to keep up with schoolwork.

Minimise the Clutter on Your Handouts: Students can be distracted not only by the clutter in their desks but also by the clutter on their papers. Simplify the visual presentation of the papers you hand out by limiting the amount of information you put on a page, or by having the student fold the paper to allow him to concentrate on one part or problem at a time. When giving a test of more than one page, consider giving the student one page at a time. Also, direct his attention to key information through highlighting or underlining.

Model the Way to Approach a Project or Assignment: Students who are disorganised can find large projects overwhelming. Just figuring out where to start can be a challenge. Walk the student through the process by having him brainstorm on paper the various steps needed to complete the project and helping him decide on the order in which they must be done. Then, have him work out a realistic schedule of when he will work on each step of the project. Suggest that he make a list of the needed materials and gather all of them before beginning. Similarly, if he is confused by an assignment, help him break it into smaller, more doable parts, and then take it one step at a time. For long-term projects, set up interim due dates for parts of the project (for example, completion of notecards) to help keep students on track.

Teach the Student How to Keep a Neat Desk: Keeping a desk neat does not come naturally to a disorganised student. He will probably need instructions on how to reduce the chaos. Bear in mind that the goal is not to have him keep his desk meticulous but rather to have him keep it neat enough so he can find what he needs with little effort. Explain in a concrete, specific way strategies for keeping a neat desk—perhaps even listing them on a poster for display. You might have him make a list, with your guidance, of the items allowed in his desk and then have him tape the list on his desk or in his notebook.

Consider implementing a "no toys" policy to lessen the clutter. Also, suggest that he write the subjects on the spines of his textbooks so he can locate them quickly. If his desk has gotten out of control and the student is overwhelmed by the prospect of cleaning it, have him dump the contents into a bag and take them to a table to sort through. Help him figure out what to do with the contents. Rarely used items might be brought home or placed on the classroom shelf. Allow him to keep in his desk a maximum of two or three silent-reading books. Train him to clear extraneous materials from his desk before he begins to work.

Build Desk-Cleaning Time into the Class Schedule: Some students will not be able to keep their desks clean unless time is set aside for this task. For students whose desks are already clean or who end early, provide enjoyable activities they can do while their classmates finish up. Build in spot checks of the students' desks— praising those who have kept them neat. Those who have not can stay in during recess to complete the cleaning job. Do not take class time to have students organise their backpacks, although you might have them clean them out as a homework assignment.

Encourage Students to Be Responsible for Their Materials: If a student forgets to bring the proper materials to class, lend him what he needs, but consider asking him for some "collateral," to be returned when he gives back the borrowed materials. Maintain a list of items students borrow and return. If a student often forgets materials, take him aside and let him know in a gentle manner that you expect him to bring the required materials to class in the future. If the problem continues, contact his parents or give him a school consequence (for example, detention or loss of part of his recess). If he is constantly losing his pencil, have him put a piece of velcro on his desk, as well as on his pencil, to help him avoid misplacing it. Conduct spot checks to see if students have the proper materials and to put them on notice that you expect them to come to class prepared.

Have a Class Discussion in Which Students Share Their Ideas about Keeping Organised: Students can be creative in coming up with ways of staying on top of school responsibilities. Have them share organisational tips with their classmates. You may find that your students are more likely to use strategies that they know other students are using. Record their suggestions and post them, or distribute them to the class.

Encourage the Student to Solve Problems with Minimal Teacher Involvement: A disorganised student can consume much of your time. Encourage him to solve the problem on his own to minimise the disruption to your teaching as well as to foster self-reliance. If he has forgotten an item needed for class, suggest that he borrow it from a classmate. If he has forgotten a pencil, tell him to get one from a "pencil stubs" box kept on your desk or near the pencil sharpener. Keep an extra textbook on your desk that a student can borrow by noting his name and the date on a sheet of paper. Let your students know that borrowed items are to be returned at the end of the period or the day.

Assign the Student a Classroom Buddy: Arrange for an especially responsible classmate to assist a student with organisational or learning problems when you are unavailable. Tell the student to first see his "buddy" if he needs help before coming to you. A variation of this is to group students at tables, with group members expected to assist others in their group who need help.

Encourage the Use of Checklists: Have the student make a checklist to keep track of school tasks he must complete. Suggest that he keep it in an accessible place, perhaps on his desk or in his binder. Show him how to put the checklist in priority order so that he tackles the most important tasks first. Also, tell him to cross out items on the list once they are completed. You can have a younger student draw pictures rather than use words as reminders.

Teach the Student Memory Aides: Suggest that he use tangible items such as a rubber band around his wrist or a note attached to his backpack to remind him of tasks he needs to do. If he has a watch with an alarm, have him set it to go off at the time of a schedule change (for example, when he needs to go to a remedial reading class). You might also develop, or have the student develop, an acronym to help him keep track of school responsibilities. For example, suggest he use the acronym PANTS to remind him of what he must bring to school every day (P = Parent notes, A = Assignments, N = Notebook, T = Textbooks, and S = Student-himself!).

Monitor the Assignment Sheets of Students with Homework Problems, and Have Parents Do the Same: If a student has a history of not completing homework, require that he come to you at the end of the period or day so you can check the accuracy of his assignment sheet and initial it. Let the parents know that you would like them to review his assignment sheet and initial it daily when they have checked that the recorded assignments have been completed and placed in his backpack. This process can be discontinued after a few weeks if the student is completing homework regularly.

Intervene When There Is a Pattern of Incomplete Assignments: Talk with the student privately to identify the source of the problem. Is he not copying down the assignments? Is he not bringing home the proper materials? Is he confused by the directions? Does he not understand the work? Does he not have enough time to complete the work because of excessive involvement in outside activities? Is he completing it, but forgetting to bring it in? If necessary, meet with the parents along with the student to work out a specific plan to correct the problem. Follow up to make sure the student is doing what he agreed to do.

Allow the Student to Experience the Consequences of His Forgetfulness: If you excuse his forgetfulness or continually bail him out, he will have little incentive to remember. Allow the student to experience the natural consequences of his behaviour— within limits. For example, if he forgets to bring in a signed permission slip allowing him to be on the safety patrol despite repeated requests, consider dropping him from this activity. At the same time, avoid keeping him from going on a class trip because he brought back the permission slip after the due date.

Praise and Reward Students for Improved Organisation: If disorganisation is a significant problem for one or more of your students, consider implementing a behaviour modification programme to spur improvement. Describe to them in a clear, concrete way the behaviours they must focus on (for example, "copies down assignments accurately for five straight days") and then assign positive consequences for their attainment (for example, an item from the school store, a classroom privilege, or a "no homework" pass). Of course, you may find that verbal praise for improved performance is sufficient to motivate some students.

Suggest Organisational Strategies for Parents to Use with Their Children: Parents play a key role in helping to organise their children. Send a letter home early in the school year to describe your classroom and homework policies, as well as the materials required by students. Include in the letter some of the following suggestions of steps they can take to help their children stay on track:

- Encourage your child to put his school materials in the same place every day.
- Ask your child daily for notes from school, or look in the part of his binder or backpack reserved for parent information.
- Establish a "homework-comes-first" policy.
- Set limits on your child's television watching.
- Tell your child that you expect him to write down all assignments.
- Have your child do the harder assignments earlier in the evening when he is most alert.
- Put up a checklist in a prominent place to remind your child of materials to be brought to school daily.
- Mark on the family calendar tests, projects, and important school activities.
- Have your child put all school materials inside his backpack before going to bed.

The following are some additional strategies for helping your students stay organised:

- Make sure your students can tell time using a nondigital clock.
- Use paper of different colours for different tasks so students can locate the papers easily.

- Have students use self-stick notes to mark the pages they are on.
- Punch holes in the handouts you give to students so they can easily put them in their binders.
- Require disorganised students to check with you before they go home, to make sure they have the proper materials and have correctly recorded assignments.

Collaborative Strategic Reading Techniques

Collaborative Strategic Reading (CSR) is an excellent technique for teaching students reading comprehension and building vocabulary and also working together cooperatively. CSR is great for kids with learning disabilities because they contribute to their groups and feel successful, and they get the help they need with their reading. Lucille Sullivan and Sallie Gotch teach heterogeneous intermediate-grade classes that include students with learning disabilities. They learned Collaborative Strategic Reading (CSR) as an instructional approach for multilevel classrooms and have been implementing it for a year or more. These teachers are enthusiastic about CSR because they believe it has improved their students' reading comprehension, increased their vocabularies, enhanced cooperative skills, and enriched content area learning. Following are the phases of how to teach CSR to students.

Phase 1: Teaching the Strategies

Students learn four strategies as part of CSR's Plan for Strategic Reading: Preview, Click and Clunk, Get the Gist, and Wrap Up. Preview is used only before reading the entire text for that lesson, and Wrap Up is used only after reading the entire text for the lesson. The other two strategies, Click and Clunk and Get the Gist, are used many times while reading the text, after each paragraph or two. In the following sections provide an overview of how to teach each of the strategies:

Preview

Students preview the entire passage before they read each section. The goals of previewing are (a) for students to learn as much about the passage as they can in a brief period of time (2-3 minutes), (b) to activate their background knowledge about the topic, and (c) to help them make predictions about what they will learn. Previewing serves to motivate students' interest in the topic and to engage them in active reading from the onset. Introduce previewing to students by asking them whether they have ever been to the movies and seen previews. Prompt students to tell you what they learn from previews by asking questions like the following:

- Do you learn who is going to be in the movie?
- Do you learn during what historical period the movie will take place?
- Do you learn whether or not you might like the movie?
- Do you have questions about what more you would like to know about the movie?

When students preview before reading, they should look at headings; words that are bolded or underlined; and pictures, tables, graphs, and other key information to help them do two things: (a) brainstorm what they know about the topic and (b) predict what they will learn about the topic. Just as in watching a movie preview, students are provided minimal time to generate their ideas and discuss their background knowledge and predictions.

Click and Clunk

Students click and clunk while reading each section of the passage. The goal of clicking and clunking is to teach students to monitor their reading comprehension and to identify when they have breakdowns in understanding. Clicks refer to portions of the text that make sense to the reader: "Click, click, click"- comprehension clicks into place as the reader proceeds smoothly through the text. When a student comes to a word, concept, or idea that does not make sense, Clunk- comprehension breaks down. For example, when students do not know the meaning of a word, it is a clunk. Many students with reading and learning problems fail to monitor their understanding when they read. Clicking and clunking is designed to teach students to pay attention to when they are understanding - or failing to understand - what they are reading or what is being read to them. The teacher asks, "Is everything clicking?

Who has clunks about the section we just read?" Students know that they will be asked this question and are alert to identify clunks during reading. After students identify clunks, the class uses "fix-up" strategies to figure out the clunks. Tiffany Royal teaches her students to use "clunk cards" as prompts to remind them of various fix-up strategies. On each of the clunk cards is printed a different strategy for figuring out a clunk word, concept, or idea:

— Reread the sentence without the word. Think about what information that is provided that would help you understand the meaning of the word.

– Reread the sentence with the clunk and the sentences before or after the clunk looking for clues.

– Look for a prefix or suffix in the word.

– Break the word apart and look for smaller words you know.

As with the other strategies, you may teach students the click and clunk strategy from the beginning of the year and use it in various contexts. Students apply these fix-up strategies at first with help from the teacher and then in their small groups.

Get the Gist

Students learn to get the gist by identifying the most important idea in a section of text (usually a paragraph). The goal of getting the gist is to teach students to restate in their own words the most important point as a way of making sure they have understood what they have read. This strategy can improve students' understanding and memory of what they have learned. When you teach students to "get the gist," prompt them to identify the most important person, place, or thing in the paragraph they have just read. Then ask them to tell you in their own words the most important idea about the person, place, or thing. Teach students to provide the gist in as few words as possible while conveying the most meaning, leaving out details.

Wrap Up

Students learn to wrap up by formulating questions and answers about what they have learned and by reviewing key ideas. The goals are to improve students' knowledge, understanding, and memory of what was read. Students generate questions that ask about important information in the passage they have just read. The best way to teach wrap up is to tell students to use the following question starters to begin their questions: who, what, when, where, why, and how (the 5 Ws and an H). It is also a good idea to tell students to pretend they are teachers and to think of questions they would ask on a test to find out if their students really understood what they had read.

Other students should try to answer the questions. If a question cannot be answered, that might mean it is not a good question and needs to be clarified. Teach students to ask some questions about information that is stated explicitly in the passage and other questions that require an answer not right in the passage, but "in your head." Encourage students to ask questions that involve higher-level thinking skills, rather than literal recall. With her fifth-grade students, Tiffany Royal emphasises that every question can be made into an even better question with the addition of the phrase, "Why do you think that?" Students write down the most important ideas they learned from the day's reading assignment in their CSR Learning Logs. They then take turns sharing what they learned with the class. Many students can share their best idea in a short period of time, providing the teacher with valuable information about each student's level of understanding.

Phase 2. Co-operative Learning Group Roles

Once students have developed proficiency applying the comprehension strategies through teacher-led activities, they are ready to learn the roles they will perform while using CSR in their peer-led cooperative learning groups.

Roles are an important aspect of CSR because cooperative learning seems to work best when all group members have been assigned a meaningful task. Roles should rotate on a regular basis so that students can experience a variety of roles and so that everyone takes a turn being the Leader. Students can perform more than one role at a time, if necessary. Possible roles include the following:

- *Leader*: This student leads the group in the implementation of CSR by saying what to read next and what strategy to apply next. The leader asks the teacher for assistance, if necessary.
- *Clunk Expert*: This student uses clunk cards to remind the group of the steps to follow when trying to figure out a difficult word or concept.
- *Announcer*: This student calls on different group members to read or share an idea. He or she makes sure everyone participates and only one person talks at a time.
- *Encouraged*: This student watches the group and gives feedback. He or she looks for behaviours to praise. The student encourages all group members to participate in the discussion and assist one another. He or she evaluates how well the group has worked together and gives suggestions for improvement.
- *Reporter*: During the whole-class wrap-up, this student reports to the class the main ideas the group learned and shares a favourite question the group has generated.
- *Time Keeper*: This student sets the timer for each portion of CSR and lets the group know when it is time to move on (the teacher might do this instead of students).

Materials

The following materials may be helpful as you assist students to use both cooperative learning techniques and comprehension strategies. For example, cue cards or sheets can be effective reminders of cooperative learning roles.

Cue Sheets

Cue sheets outline the procedures to be followed in cooperative learning groups and provide structure and support for students while they are learning CSR. Each role comes with a corresponding cue sheet that explains the steps to be followed to fulfil that role. Cue sheets seem to help students stay focused and on task, and increase their confidence. Students should discontinue use of the cue sheets when they feel secure in carrying out their roles.

CSR Learning Logs

CSR learning logs enable students to keep track of learning "as it happens" and provide a springboard for follow-up activities. Logs furnish an additional way for all students to participate actively in their groups. Logs can be used for recording ideas while applying every strategy, or only used for some of the strategies (e.g., for writing down clunks and key ideas). Logs might be kept in spiral-bound notebooks or journals made by folding paper in half and stapling on a construction paper cover. You may create a different learning log for each social studies or science unit; these logs provide written documentation of learning and become excellent study guides. Some special education teachers have even used CSR learning logs to document that students were meeting the objectives on their individualised education programmes (IEPs).

Reading Materials

CSR was designed primarily to be used with expository text found in social studies and other content area textbooks, yet CSR can also be used with narrative text. You should select reading material with well-formed, interesting passages that are conducive to strategy application. Such material is characterised by the following:

- Providing clues that help students predict what they will be learning.
- Having one main idea in a paragraph.
- Providing context that helps students connect information.

We recommend that when you begin CSR you use the Weekly Reader, Junior Scholastic, or a similar nonfiction publication that captures students' interest and can be read in a short time.

Timer

A timer is optional. Kitchen timers that students set by themselves can help groups to remain on task and not get excessively bogged down with anqy one strategy or step in the CSR process. For example, the timekeeper might say, "We have 10 minutes to write down everything we already know about the topic." Then the timekeeper would set the timer for 10 minutes. An alternative is for the teacher to set one timer and direct students in their groups to carry out the strategies for a set period of time. We recommend using this procedure for at least the first few days that students work together in groups so that they can develop an understanding of how the process works. Yet once groups can function more autonomously, they should be encouraged to do so.

Teacher's Role in Monitoring Groups

Once you have taught the strategies and procedures to students and they have begun working in their cooperative learning groups, your role is to circulate among the groups and provide ongoing assistance. You can help by actively listening to students' conversations and if necessary clarifying difficult words, modelling strategy usage, encouraging students to participate, and modelling a helpful attitude. It is expected that students will need assistance learning to work in cooperative groups, implementing the strategies, and mastering academic content.

Understanding of Textbook Content

The three-phase textbook teaching and learning model, is based on cognitive learning theory and offers both special and general educators a new set of practices to utilise so that students with reading disabilities will be more effectively involved in textbook learning. The model has a wide range of applicability which could potentially reduce the memory demands on students. It involves showing students how they may best learn the new content in three phases: before reading, during reading, and after reading. The following three phases and some teaching suggestions for each phase.

Phase I: Before reading

Instead, spark students' interest by activating prior

knowledge and by focusing on the purpose of reading. The time spent in Phase I activities can be viewed as a "head start" and a chance to get students thinking and to spark interest and curiosity in the upcoming topic. Following are the suggestions for Phase I:

- *Select core vocabulary*: These are words students will likely encounter again or those which are germane to the main idea of the lesson. Present the terms on the board or on paper and ask students to write the definition, if only a guess. Collect and return at the end of Phase III to complete by filling in the correct responses.
- *Written predictions*: This technique involves the readers by asking them to make guesses about what they think they will learn from reading the passage and what they would like to learn related to the topic.
- *Analogies and visual images*: This pre-reading strategy helps students make meaningful links between what they will be learning and what is familiar to them. This conjures up mental "pictures" which can help students organise new information which is easier for retention and recall. For example, if the class was about to read a passage regarding a typical school day in Japan, the teacher could lead a discussion to review familiar information about which the students already have — a typical school day in the United States. Teachers should continue to reinforce this type of analogous thinking because it demonstrates that while the students may have poor reading skills they are developing their ability to think abstractly.
- *Concept maps*: Many teachers are aware of the value of presenting information in a visual format such as the concept map. Used before reading, concept maps can

show students the important concepts and ideas of the chapter and how they are related to one another. Maps can be completed or partially completed so that they fill in the remaining concepts as they are studied.

The teacher's job is to decide which of these techniques is most appropriate given the material to be read and her knowledge of the students. Phase I pre-reading strategies will set the stage for the learners to be more interested in the new content and to be confident in their ability to understand the lesson which is about to be presented.

Phase II: During Reading

Lecture followed by oral or silent reading is not enough for students with reading disabilities because:

- poor readers expend much energy and time struggling with individual words rather than constructing meaning from the text;
- they overattend to individual words and are less able to utilise the context to predict meaning; and
- many textbooks are organised so that main ideas are embedded and too many concepts are treated superficially. Following are the suggestions for phase II:
- *Reciprocal teaching techniques*: This is a powerful technique because students assume more dominant roles in the learning process. Teachers and students become partners in constructing meaning from the text. This technique generally takes about ten days to teach. During this instructional period, the teacher provides a great deal of modelling. The students eventually assume the role of teacher/leader in summarising the content and leading a discussion with the other

students. During the discussion period, students may ask the teacher/leader for clarification of terms or key points made in the text.

- *Insert*: This is an active reading technique which calls for the reader to interact with and respond to the text as he reads. This is particularly useful when the student is completing a home reading assignment. It helps the student to become more aware of any breakdown in his comprehension and provides a way for him to remember to clarify any ambiguity at a later point, like the next day in class. The technique calls for the student to mark in his book (if he owns it) or on 1 inch × 1-1/2 inch "stickies" as he reads to record his thoughts about points made in the passage. For example, if the student doesn't understand a particular passage, he might put question marks on the "stickie" and attach it next to the passage. The student can develop his own system of codes for interacting with the text.

- *Mapping strategies*: Like reciprocal teaching, this strategy should be taught and modelled for the students. Mapping can be more appealing than the traditional note taking because it combines visual or graphic symbols with words.

- *Short summary notes*: Students can be taught a technique for condensing the main ideas and important supporting details of a chapter by using a tool which assists them in organising the key points. The teacher "chunks" the reading passages for the students and asks them to record the main ideas and supporting details for each passage on a frame. The students place the title of the passage in the centre of the summary frame, two to four main ideas in circles around the title and one to three details under each main idea.

- *Transactional strategy instruction*: Emphasis here is not only on teaching a variety of strategies to improve students' academic growth but to lengthen students' commitment to learning. It involves taking them through understanding the nature of the strategies and making decisions about the best time to utilise them. Therefore, the students are actively involved in choosing the learning strategy for the task.

Phase III: After Reading

Traditional questions and paper-pencil tests are not sufficient ways to help students retain new knowledge. Following are the suggestions for phase III:

- *Vocabulary/prediction*: Redistribute the vocabulary or written prediction forms from Phase I. Have students fill in the final column which asks them what they know now, after reading the chapter. Have students examine the shift in their thinking from the pre-reading level to the post-reading level.
- *Analyse end-of-the-chapter questions*: Use these questions as a review of the type of questions that are generally asked in textbooks – those looking for factual answers; those asking them to make an inference or analysis; or those asking their opinion. Teach students to discriminate among the three types. Do not require the students to answer the questions; build their ability to think and analyse.
- *Good/bad examples of writing*: Rather than have students give one word answers to questions at the end of the chapter, have them view, analyse, and discuss good and bad examples of chapter summaries. Review what makes the examples good and bad. Then have them

write their own chapter summary using the same criteria that they applied during the "good/bad activity", and have the students exchange and edit each others' summaries.

– *Recreational reading of topics that relate to textbook*: Provide students other resources to read that relate to the textbook. This can provide opportunities for a great source of growth in vocabulary, spelling, and writing. Trade books or magazines on the readers' independent reading level should be readily available in class and self-selected by the reader, and available.

The textbook continues to be a heavily relied upon tool in schools today, especially at the secondary level. There is no research to support the traditional method of assigning textbook reading, lecturing, and asking questions, yet a significant number of teachers still subscribe to this routine. We need to more actively engage the students in the learning process at every possible opportunity – before reading, while reading, and after reading in order to increase their comprehension and long-term retention.

Study Skills Instruction

Study skills instruction develops in students a metacognitive approach to school - they learn how to learn. Students need to go beyond completing an assignment and think about how they complete it. They need to be aware of the process they follow and steps they take when prereading a textbook, taking notes in class, or answering an essay question on a test. To most people, teaching basic skills means the 3 R's: Reading, wRiting and aRithmetic. Study skills are an essential component of basic skills which for too long has been neglected. Study skills instruction benefits all students, but it is crucial to students who have learning disabilities. Study skills instruction gives students the "tools" and the "training" they need to do a good job in school.

The more adept a student is with reading, writing, speaking and study skills, the more efficient and thorough he or she will be at getting the job of learning done. Too often, however, we move children through the grades without sufficient tools or training. As students progress through each stage of education, they must develop a new set of skills to cope with greater demands. In the primary grades, they learn to read and write and organise themselves. From third to sixth grade, the emphasis switches to reading and writing to learn, and assumptions are made about how organised students should be at this point. In junior high school, students are expected to work more independently and to keep up with increasingly difficult schedules for school work, sports, activities, and social commitments.

Upon entering high school and then college, even greater demands are placed on the student to process a more complex and increasing volume of material, and to complete more long-term assignments. The greater the demands of the grade level, the more need there is for study skills to cope with those demands. Most teachers agree that study skills are important, but many are not really sure what study skills are and whose responsibility it is to see that they are taught. College teacher-training and certification requirements usually do not include course work in the area of study skills. Curriculums are often quite detailed when it comes to content classes, and schools carefully examine these curriculums to determine which reading series or textbooks they will use across the system. Not so with study skills; for too long it has been the Cinderella of curriculum planning.

Most schools do not offer study skills instruction as part of the regular curriculum. There is often an assumption on the part of teachers and even parents that students have been taught these skills in previous grades or developed them on their own. Through no fault of their own, the higher the grade level, the less likely teachers are to include study skills instruction in lesson planning. In fact, many students are capable of developing their own systems for organising, processing and comprehending what they have read or heard in class, planning homework and longterm assignments, studying for tests, and determining good test-taking strategies. Most students who complete college have never taken study skills classes, yet they have the intact learning processes to create the necessary organisational and study strategies to be successful in their college classes.

Study Skills Model

The model begins with the development of organisation strategies, including organisation of materials, homework and longterm assignments; time-planning on a daily, weekly and monthly basis; and organisation of study space. The model then presents main idea, note taking, and summarising skills which can be taught and practiced in grades four through high school. These basic skills then become the foundation for building textbook, test-preparation and test-taking skills.

Organisation skills

It is easy to assume that students, especially in the upper

grades, have adequate organisation skills. Yet many students do not know what supplies they should bring to class, how to use an assignment pad, or how to determine how long it will take to complete an assignment. Surprising as it may seem, some very bright teenagers do not even know how to use a calendar or a nondigital clock. Teachers should spend time in class to teach students how to set up notes and materials, use assignment pads, use longterm class calendars and personal weekly calendars, and organise study space. Teachers should also:

- Help students independently apply organisation skills by explaining the rationale behind the skills
- Treat organisation skills as part of the regular curriculum
- Model the use of calendar, assignment pads and homework time sheets in class
- Clearly state expectations for the application of organisation strategies, and consistently check to see if students are meeting those expectations
- Organise and clearly explain all assignments and classwork to avoid confusion about what is required

Main idea skills

The ability to recognise and formulate main ideas is crucial for success in school, and in many ways it is a life skill. Supermarkets stock their products in the "main idea" sections of produce, bakery, dairy, etc. Even the nightly television news is presented in order of"main idea" segments such as national news, local news, sports, weather and human interest stories. Information in school that must be learned from textbooks, lectures, class discussions and filmstrips can be categorised by main ideas to organise the material and make it more accessible to the student. A main idea can be the category for a list of items, the topic of a paragraph, the theme of an essay, the topic of a textbook chapter, or the thesis of a term paper.

Main idea skills can be applied at a very basis categorising level in the second or third grade; they can also be used to organise complex information from a college textbook. In lengthier material, main ideas can be listed in a hierarchy consisting of major and secondary main ideas. There are four-step progression for introducing main idea skills:

- Categorising lists of terms or new vocabulary
- Identifying and highlighting main ideas in paragraphs that have topic sentences
- Inferring main ideas in paragraphs that do not state the main idea and formulating them in the student's own words
- Identifying main ideas in multi-paragraph selections

Teachers should introduce main ideas using simple, structured material. As the student develops the skill, it should be practiced in more complex material from a variety of subject areas.

Note taking skills

Note taking is a procedure for recording information from lectures or reading in order to learn that information and retrieve it later to study. Note taking is also a valuable tool for gathering and organising pieces of research for a report. Taking notes encourages students to be more active learners by processing information and writing it in their own words. Given that note taking requires the integration of listening, interpreting, sequencing and recording skills, it is easy to see why many students with learning disabilities feel overwhelmed when they must take notes. The two-column method of note taking, in which main ideas are listed on the left side of a page and details on the right, is the best technique for introducing and developing note taking skills.

The L.S.S. Model introduces note taking by following the same four-step progression used with main idea skills. Note taking from lectures and other non written material should be taught after the student can confidently take notes from written sources. Teachers should also be aware that some students need to develop note taking sub-skills such as learning how to abbreviate, employing word economy, using visual markers and editing notes.

Summarising skills

Summarising helps students identify and organise the essence of the material they must learn. Sometimes there is so much information that students get lost in the details; constructing a summary enables them to see the greater picture. By searching for main ideas and relevant details, students become active readers and listeners. Reprocessing the information to produce a summary in their own words also provides practice for expressing that knowledge on a test or in class discussion. Two-column notes can be used for the basis of a simple summary.

The main ideas in the left column form an outline; the students turn these into sentences to write a summary. As with main idea skills, teachers should introduce summarising using structured, simple material and progressing to lengthy, more complex material. Summarising should also be practiced using a variety of subject matter; summaries from history material can be quite different than summaries from science material. Writing summaries from literary sources, such as short stories, is a good way to recall the key characters and sequence of events. Such a summary then becomes the basis of a book or story report. Consistently assigning students the task of summarising notes, readings and class lectures trains them to apply good review skills.

Personal management skills

Teachers and parents believe that doing homework helps students take responsibility for themselves and develops character and personal management skills. The significant role of homework is underscored by the finding that homework accounts for about 20% of the time students spend on academic tasks. Because homework accounts for one-fifth of the time that successful students are engaged in academic tasks and because so many students in both general and special education programmes experience problems, we must help students acquire skills for doing schoolwork at home. The classroom teacher assigns and evaluates homework, but students complete it in environments over which the teacher has no control. Thus, addressing homework problems requires teamwork-by teachers, students, and parents.

Success of homework strategies

First, evaluate your own practices. Teachers sometimes

underestimated the amount of time it took students to complete assignments; the assignments may have been too difficult for some and too easy for others, and there was little consistency in homework assignments from class to class even in the same grade in the school. Here are some effective ways to assess your own practice:

– Jot down how long you think an assignment should take students to complete. Ask students to indicate on a corner of their completed work how long it took to complete. Examine whether there is a match between your expectations and students reports. The student who takes much longer than expected may not have understood the assignment, may not know how to do it, may have attention problems, or may have distractions at home. Your assignment also may have been much more difficult than you assumed.

– Put smiley, frowning, and neutral faces on the corner of assignments. Have students circle the one that describes their feelings about the assignments (e.g., it was too easy, too hard, or just right). Use students responses in a discussion. Provide students with your rationale for doing (unpopular) assignments, or consider changing assignments.

– Talk to other teachers in your school about their homework assignments. Try to reach consensus about the length and frequency of assignments. Special education teachers often do not want to burden their students with homework. Not giving assignments to students with special needs, however, may result in their spending significantly less time doing schoolwork and in acquiring independent study skills.

Innovative homework assignments

- Work with other teachers to adopt similar practices. For instance, develop a standard style for homework headings. This reduces the need to teach students how to head their papers every year.
- Use games and fun activities as home work assignments. Teachers in our study found many games and activities that were not only fun, but also reinforced the principles they were trying to teach. Students can make these activities in class (e.g., games like Go Fish and Concentration) and take them home to play with other family members. Older students can do oral-histories and interview family members or others involved in events related to their studies (e.g., earthquakes, war).
- Effective assignments are relevant to the child's life outside of the class room. Help children make the connection between what they learn in school and their lives outside of in school. For example, use the newspapers TV listings and children's favourite television programmes to help children learn how to tell time. Home chores and projects are also good sources of effective homework. For example, have students measure walls at home and estimate the cost of painting them; keep track of money spent on groceries; or estimate the amount of ingredients necessary to make their favourite foods. Games and relevant assignments help develop the under standing that learning takes place everywhere, and that our children are capable of learning everywhere. These activities provide pleasant ways to involve other family members in the child's schoolwork.

– Give students rewards for homework completion. Ask students to select possible rewards. One class asked to make up cheers, and to do the cheers.

Homework planner

Independent learners acquire self-monitoring skills. As adults we learn to use calendars or other aids such as notes to selfmonitor our activities. We record and track the various events in our lives, important dates, tasks and chores, meetings and plans. Many students can benefit from using such structured notes.

Use a homework planner to help students acquire organisational skills. Students need to be shown how to use the planner-which can be a small calendar, with pages divided into sections. Demonstrate where to write assignments, how to write them in shorthand, how to note that their assignments have been completed. Help students identify study times by filling in their other activities (e.g., meal times, scout activities).

IF use the planner to communicate with parents. Ask parents to sign it when assignments have been completed. Invite them to send you messages about how well their children did on the assignment. Use the planner to send brief messages home to parents.

Show students how to graph their homework completion in the planner. In the study, students used Magic Markers to colour green for completed assignments, yellow for late assignments, and red for assignments not turned in. Yellow became green or red depending on the childs followup. A sea of red ink speaks loud and clear to parents about their children's failure to complete homework assignments. A sea of green ink is cause for celebration.

Teach study skills

Many students need to learn study skills. We developed the "Sequenced Study Skills Programme" to teach the following.

- *Basic Strategies*: Identifying a time and place for doing homework, having the necessary materials, placing completed work in a safe spot, remembering to bring it to school, and reducing distractions generated by other family members, pets, or television.
- *Metacognitive Skills*: Monitoring the impact of television viewing and other distractions on time to do homework, recognising signs of fatigue and lack of attention, and developing methods to cope with fatigue and lack of attention.
- *Specific Study Skills*: Taking notes, using strategies to increase reading comprehension, and using mnemonics as memory helpers.

Work with Parents

- Parents are much more likely to be supportive of your efforts if they have a clear understanding of your expectations, rules, and standards regarding homework.
- Let parents know how much homework you plan to assign, and approximately how long assignments should take.
- If there is a discrepancy between the child's performance and your expectations, treat this as diagnostic information. If you have informed the parents about what you expect of the child, the parents can be part of the solution by providing descriptive

data concerning what happens at home during homework time. Sometimes the solution requires parent intervention, such as when other siblings are interfering with the homework process. Sometimes the solution requires that you adapt assignments to the child's capabilities, such as giving less or different homework. Sometimes the solution focuses on the child, such as when the child fails to bring home assignments or tells the parent there are no assignments.

– Suggest activities that parents can do with their children. Games and activities that the whole family can participate in, that can be done in the car or waiting in the doctors office, or that are part of grocery shopping are effective ways to increase students learning time.

– See if the parents feel comfortable working on schoolwork with the child. For example, some parents might read aloud to children or drill them for quizzes. Students can also read aloud to parents.

– Ask the parent to play the role of student and have the child play the role of teacher. Explaining concepts to others is one of the best ways of learning the concept.

– Ask the parent to sign completed homework. Invite the parent to write short notes about how well the child is doing. Parents complain that they are not aware that their children are doing badly until parent-teacher conference time or until they receive report cards. Signing homework and exchanging short notes are frequently effective in alerting both parents and teachers that the child is experiencing problems. Early warnings allow time to address the problem before it is too late in the school year.

- Encourage parents to talk to the child about what happened during the school day. For example, during dinner, each member of the family can take turns relating what they did that day. Model positive responses for parents; for example, So you worked hard and really got it!
- Encourage the parent to reward the child for homework completion. Rewards can be small treats, but they go a long way in defining schoolwork as important.

When children fail to complete their homework or do an unacceptable job, enlist parents support in solving the problem. Keep in mind that some parents feel that criticisms of their children reflect badly on their parenting skills. You must establish rapport with parents if you expect to engage their help in solving the problem.

- Meet with the parent. Be positive; say nice things about the child.
- Acknowledge the problem. Ask for the parent's assessment of the problem.
- Listen carefully and take notes. Record positive and negative descriptors.
- Ask the parent to keep a log or develop a checklist of what happens at home around homework time. Parents who, get home late from work may not be able, or willing, to do this. It would help to have objective descriptions of what is taking place so as to distinguish between problems caused by the child (e.g., attention problems), by the school (e.g., assignments that are too difficult or long), or by the family setting (e.g., sibling interference).

- Based on the parents input, develop a strategy for solving the problem. Select one behaviour to change and one strategy to try. Be specific about who is going to do what and when.
- Set a date for the next meeting and follow through. Check on the effectiveness of the strategy. Choose another behaviour or another strategy. Be sure to follow through.

Peer support

Peers are a potent source of child influence that often are overlooked. Peers can help students who are having homework problems. Here are some effective ways to harness positive peer influence.

- Establish BuddyStudy pairs or cooperative groups.
- Teach students how to work together. Coach them on how to take turns practising skills being learned, how to quiz each other, how to correct each others work, and how to say nice things to each other.
- Give students assignments and have them meet for about 10 minutes at the beginning and end of class. Students check each others (a) understanding of the assignment and (b) completion of the assignment. Team members help each other correct their home work papers.
- Record the completion and accuracy of homework assignments.
- Give students points for completion and accuracy. Add team members scores, and give a special reward to those who meet a specified criterion (e.g., 80% correct).
- Let teams graph their scores each week.

Homework requires a set of skills that are not directly taught by parents and teachers. Yet the skills involved in doing homework, such as time management and organisational strategies, are important well beyond school years. Corporations and adults continue to seek methods to improve their skills, often at considerable personal cost. Teachers and parents intuit students needs to develop these skills. Teachers can do much to help students assume responsibility for their own learning, and to acquire these basic, lifelong skills.

4

Teaching of History

History provides a distinctive education by providing a sense of the past, an awareness of the development of differing values, systems and societies and the inculcation of critical yet tolerant personal attitudes. The concepts, theories and methodologies of the social sciences are themselves used by many historians, most obviously but by no means exclusively within courses in economic and social history. There has been a long and important tradition in the United Kingdom of teaching and writing history within a social science framework, which continues both within distinct degree programmes in economic and social history and as an important feature in many degree programmes in History.

Where history is taught within the context of the social sciences, students will need to devote considerable time to acquiring a knowledge of one or more social science. In general, students of all types of history—cultural and political as well as economic and social—should have an awareness of relevant and appropriate concepts and theories. Particular types of skill, quality, and accomplishment are not connected solely to particular types of course provision or subject matter. Just as there is no one model for a programme, there will be no one model for the relationship between course provision and students' attainments.

Good undergraduate history teaching takes a variety of forms, and programmes quite legitimately combine different teaching methods in a number of ways. This variety arises from the different interests and abilities of individual scholars, from the requirements of different areas of the field of history, and from the fact that departments or subject groups in different institutions have access to different combinations of teaching resources. Assessment is a critical element in the educational process and an essential element in effective learning.

Therefore all departments should develop a clear assessment policy which is consistent with the learning outcomes of its degree schemes. They should specify clearly in their documentation what students are expected to learn, how their work will be assessed, and the relationship between the two. Departments should think carefully about and explain the relationship between the functions of formative and summative assessment, ie between assessment designed as feedback on progress and assessment for degree award and classification purposes.

Important abilities and qualities of mind are acquired through the study of History. They are particularly valuable for the graduate as citizen and are readily transferable to many occupations and careers. Some of these qualities and abilities are generic, in that they are imparted by most degree programmes in the Humanities and Social Sciences. But degree- level study in History also instils ways of thinking which are intrinsic to the discipline while being no less transferable. These include a respect for historical context and evidence, a greater awareness of the historical processes unfolding in our own time, and a deeper understanding of the varied traditions current today. These qualities of mind and abilities are most effectively and economically developed by deep and prolonged immersion in, and engagement with, the practice, methods and material of the subject itself.

The cumulative acquisition of, and ability to apply transferable skills, and the development of students as competent historians thus necessarily proceed hand-in-hand. The link between the two lies ultimately in the habits of mind or intellectual approach developed by students who have been trained as capable practising historians. These will continue to inform the application of their minds to other matters later in life. History programmes do not impart knowledge and skills to be passively absorbed: reading, discussion and writing, and engagement, exploration and discovery are essential. The historian's skills and qualities of mind are developed through the processes of acquiring, evaluating and discussing historical knowledge in the courses and the independent study that History degree programmes demand.

The learning outcomes of a history degree programme have to be seen in terms of particular pieces of student work—either written or spoken—in which crucial tests are understanding texts and marshalling an argument. Accordingly, the ability to deploy ideas and information, to show conceptual grasp and to shape argument becomes difficult to separate in assessment practice from the ability to display appropriately relevant, wide and diverse historical knowledge. History degree students should undertake programmes which foster and inculcate the following skills and qualities:

i. The ability to understand how people have existed, acted and thought in the always different context of the past. History involves the cultural shock of encountering and sensing the past's otherness and of learning to understand unfamiliar structures, cultures and belief systems. These forms of understanding also shed important light on the influence which the past has on the present.

ii. The ability to read and use texts and other source materials, both critically and empathetically, while addressing questions of genre, content, perspective and purpose.

iii. The appreciation of the complexity and diversity of situations, events and past mentalities. This emphasis is central to History's character as an anti-reductionist discipline fostering intellectual maturity.

iv. The understanding of the problems inherent in the historical record itself: awareness of a range of viewpoints and the way to cope with this; appreciation of the range of problems involved in the interpretation of complex, ambiguous, conflicting and often incomplete material; a feeling for the limitations of knowledge and the dangers of simplistic explanations.

v. Basic critical skills: a recognition that statements are not all of equal validity, that there are ways of testing them, and that historians operate by rules of evidence which, though themselves subject to critical evaluation, are also a component of intellectual integrity and maturity.

vi. Intellectual independence: a History programme is not simply or even primarily a preparation for research in the subject, but it should incorporate the general skills of the researcher, namely the ability to set tasks and solve problems. This involves: bibliographic skills; the ability to gather, sift, select, organise and synthesise large quantities of evidence; the ability to formulate appropriate questions and to provide answers to them using valid and relevant evidence and argument. It should develop reflexivity, ie an understanding of the nature of the discipline including what questions are asked by historians, and why.

vii. Marshalling of argument—in written and oral form drawing on and presenting all the above skills.

Such argument should have structure; it should be relevant and concise. In the case of written argument it should be expressed in clear, lucid and coherent prose. Orally it should involve the capacity to sustain a reasoned line of argument in the face of others, to listen, to engage in sustained debate, and amend views as necessary in the light of evidence and argument. Some programmes, e.g. in economic and social history, incorporate the methodologies of other Humanities and Social Science disciplines.

A number of specific skills are thus essential to particular types of programme, and desirable though not obligatory in others. Departments or institutions are strongly recommended to make provision, where appropriate, for the development of at least one of these: languages; the use of Computer and IT in learning or analysis; numeracy and quantitative methods; archaeological fieldwork; archival study; or skills associated with the study of other disciplines with which

History has close links. The generic skills acquired through the study of History are:

i. Self-discipline;

ii. Self-direction;

iii. Independence of mind, and initiative;

iv. Ability to work with others, and have respect for others' reasoned views;

v. Ability to gather, organise and deploy evidence, data and information; and familiarity with appropriate means of identifying, finding, retrieving, sorting and exchanging information;

vi. Analytical ability, and the capacity to consider and solve problems, including complex problems.

vii. Structure, coherence, clarity and fluency of oral expression;

viii. Structure, coherence, clarity and fluency of written expression;

ix. Intellectual integrity and maturity;

x. Empathy and imaginative insight;

History provision across the sector is characterised by a diversity of periods, cultures, methodologies and conceptual assumptions. Nevertheless a number of central requirements can be specified. These six requirements do not point to a particular combination of courses or a particular programme structure:

- *Time depth*: Awareness of continuity and change over an extended time-span is central to an historical awareness. It leads to an understanding of historical process, and it opens the way to the insights which stem from a juxtaposition of past and present.

Programmes should introduce students to the issues of continuity and change and give them experience of the intellectual benefits accruing from the study of History over an extended period of past time. Programmes which cover a relatively short time-span should demonstrate how they provide students with a long-term perspective on their subject-matter.

– *Geographical range*: For good reasons it has become an established convention that students study the history of more than one society or culture. Among other things this opens the way to comparative perspectives. Where a single country is the focus of the programme, that programme should incorporate serious and sustained comparison with others. The student whose prime interest lies in Britain is in no way exempt from this requirement: the possibilities of enhanced objectivity which flow from studying other countries are particularly important, not to mention the implications of Britain's imperial past and multicultural present. History's ability to promote understanding between cultures and between national traditions remains as important as ever.

– *Contemporary sources*: Opportunity for close work on source material originating in the period studied is essential. This will often comprise written documents, but when appropriate will include artefacts, visual evidence etc. Students should carry out intensive critical work on such source material. This may take place in a "Special Subject" course, in other courses or in independent work. In many instances the work done by students approximates to historical research.

– *Reflexivity*: All History students should be expected to reflect critically on the nature of their discipline, its social rationale, its theoretical underpinnings and its intellectual standing. This may take place in a course labelled historigraphy or historical method, in other courses or in independent work.

– *Diversity of specialisms*: History comprises many varieties, each with its distinctive focus and theoretical orientation (for instance, economic, social, political, cultural, environmental history, the history of women, and gender). Students should be introduced to some of these varieties of approach. The aim is not comprehensiveness, but a critical awareness that there are many principles of selection and modes of enquiry. Where a programme is strongly based on one variety, serious comparisons must be made with the contribution of others to historical understanding.

– *An extended piece of written work*: This allows the student to formulate, execute and complete an independent extended piece of written work with appropriate supervision. In most cases this will be based on contemporary source materials. Alternatively it may take the form of an in-depth historiographical enquiry, as in the critical evaluation of a particular historical controversy. It may be free-standing, or it may arise from—and be linked to—a taught course. Where this is not offered at all, departments should demonstrate and justify an alternative and commensurate experience of work in depth.

Students progress through History degree programmes largely by gaining experience and knowledge as they take successive courses over a period normally of three—four years. It is a cumulative process of "learning by doing". Subject matter varies, and courses may make heavier and/or more sophisticated demands on students over time, but the general process is one of developing and reinforcing similar skills and qualities throughout the programme. Qualitative advances may be achieved in a number of ways, for instance through increasing conceptual sophistication, increasing interpretative skill, increasing capacity for sustained written and/or oral analysis, greater independence of learning, and so on.

Departments are not therefore expected to conform to any one model, but they should show how their particular programmes are designed to provide students with the means to gain in insight, competence and performance over years. Some programmes may in effect give students nine terms (or six semesters) of doing the same kind of thing with a variety of subject matter but with a growing competence. Others may attach particular skills and attributes to particular courses and prescribe how students shall move through them.

Whatever the structure of the programme, students are expected to achieve higher standards at the end of their degree studies than at the beginning; departments will need to show how their particular programme facilitates this process. Because History is a non-sequential discipline, there is no fixed order of progression from one type of course to another. There is no reason in principle why survey courses should be more strongly represented in year 1, or close documentary study in year 3, if departments are able to demonstrate how their particular provision fosters progression. Students should be provided with documentation for each individual course which explains what the course is designed to achieve, and the means to its attainment.

Documents should also include an outline of the course structure, information about the nature and amount of assessment, and a bibliography. These course guides should be designed to be read by students in relation to departmental documentation which includes details of the degree scheme, criteria for all levels of classification and all forms of assessment in use, the range of available courses, course structures, assessment methods and weightings, and advice about plagiarism. Both individual course and departmental documentation should make the teaching and learning available to students in as clear and straightforward a form as possible. Programmes should offer students regular formal contact with tutors and other students in a variety of structured settings.

The purpose of these engagements is to deepen their research, oral and communication skills. They should also inculcate the qualities of self-discipline, which are necessary for the successful pursuit of the discipline. The precise form and nature of these engagements within departments will, to some extent, be shaped by circumstances. But they will need to be the result of an internal planning process which determines and reviews the match between standard learning outcomes for the degree and the content and teaching/assessment methods employed in the department's individual courses and degree programmes.

It is vital to note that teaching methods/learning opportunities should not be thought of as fixed categories. They must be kept under review by departments, with due consideration being given for instance to tutors' self-assessments, student course review questionnaires, and the dissemination of good practice from other departments and institutions. There should be opportunities in the degree scheme for all students to experience lecture or lecture-type arrangements which capture their interest and excite their curiosity.

Presentations by lecturers stamp the course or subject with the imprint of personality and enable students to reflect on and to respond to an individual's particular interpretative approach. Lectures provide a broad framework which helps define the course, while also introducing students to its main themes, debates and interpretations. At their best they offer direct entry into a range of information and ideas which students may never, or only very rarely, be able to gather for themselves; they thus serve as a launching-pad into the heart of new subject matter. They should enable the students to develop their skills in listening, selective note-taking, and reflection.

Lectures will be more appropriate to certain kinds of courses than to others and it is for course teams to decide on their optimum deployment. There should be a requirement during the degree scheme for all students to engage in seminars and forms of group work. In these sessions students should be expected to participate in group discussion, give presentations and jointly explore themes and arguments. These group discussions should be aimed at improving students' understanding rather than at the acquisition of knowledge per se and should be structured in such a way as to maximise effective student participation. They will normally be preceded by a prescribed programme of reading. Such work should be seen as both deepening students' understanding of a theme or subject and developing oral communication skills. It encourages a critical, as well as self-critical but tolerant, approach to historical discussion and builds students' self-confidence. It improves their abilities to marshal historical evidence and to summarise historical arguments, as well as to think quickly on their feet, to communicate articulately and persuasively with others and to recognise the value of working closely with others.

Most of a history student's time is spent working independently, reading, thinking and writing. Course bibliographies and other reading advice will provide students with the necessary starting points, but they should be encouraged by tutors to make imaginative use of the library, the web etc. to expand their knowledge base and their range of historical approaches. History is largely a text-based discipline which requires students to learn to read widely, rapidly and critically, to take good notes, to digest arguments and to synthesise information quickly and intelligently. It also requires them to construct arguments in writing.

Students should be expected to undertake a wide range of assignments. It should be explained to students how such assignments enable them to improve their writing and oral-communication skills, as well as those of evidence-handling, the critical treatment of themes/ historical arguments and the thoughtful, persuasive presentation of their work. Assignments should be appropriate to the aims and intended outcomes of the course, though equity in the treatment of students and a balanced range of assessment across the whole programme must remain important considerations. All students should receive critical and constructive comment on their progress as an integral part of teaching and learning. There should be adequate discussion of, and response to, a student's individual work.

As a basic minimum, all tutors should specify in writing a period or periods each week while a given course is being taught when they will be available for academic consultation. Individual encounters with tutors, whether as part of a regular teaching arrangement, feedback on written work or more occasional meetings, are essential to helping students clarify areas of confusion and gain a better understanding of their own performance as well as of historical themes and issues.

Diversity in Assessment

Diversity in assessment is vital for two main reasons. First, the full range of a student's abilities is most unlikely to be revealed through any single mode. Second, the increasingly diverse educational background and formal qualifications presented on entry suggest that the degree programme should afford all students the opportunity to show what they know, understand and can do. Assessment of undergraduate performance is diverse. However, the essay remains a central component. The essay is a piece of written work in response to a particular question or issue, done either under examination conditions or as coursework.

Essays require students to demonstrate a number of skills in combination. Because of the integrative high-order skills which they develop, they are an essential element of all History assessment at this level. All single-honours students should be assessed in significant part on their essay-writing skills. All departments should give serious consideration to the provision of opportunity for single-honours students to be assessed by essays of various types. Departments give serious consideration to requiring students to write at least some essays under exam conditions which afford safeguards against plagiarism and the use of inappropriate outside assistance. This also gives students the opportunity to develop relevant life-skills such as the ability to produce coherent, reasoned and supported arguments under pressure.

All single honours students should be assessed in some way or another on their understanding of and their ability to handle primary source material. They should be assessed on their ability to address historical problems in depth. Students should have the chance to pursue a historical enquiry, sustaining and developing it through several stages. Such an exercise involves both task-setting and problem-solving. This is normally done through an extended piece of written work, usually of at least twice the length required for standard coursework essays. Departments should also consider whether single-honours students should be given the opportunity to have their critical and communication skills assessed in other forms.

The development of oral communication skills is important in the process of educating a historian and students should, where practicable, have opportunity to be assessed on this skill. Oral presentations can be of different types including, for example, formal paper delivered to a group; general contribution to seminar discussion; chairing or otherwise leading seminar discussion, and response to contributions made by others. All departments give serious consideration to ensuring that single honours students also have the opportunity to have their critical and communication skills assessed in some of the following ways:

i. team working and collaborative activity: group projects, fact-finding, evidence- processing work, etc;

ii. shorter written tasks, including historical literature reviews and reports;

iii. use of information technology to answer questions about historical data, including statistical and/or graphical analysis of historical data sets and to present findings in a variety of appropriate forms (bar graphs, pie charts, etc);

iv. use of information technology for bibliographic and archive searches;

v. practical experience in the use of archival material.

Establishing criteria for classification is the business of departments and institutions. Different modes of assessment will be appropriate to different schemes of study, and will reflect the particular emphases and concentrations in those programmes. In order properly to evaluate the range of undergraduate study, an honours degree in history should be awarded on the basis of more than one form of assessment. Departments should operate, and publish to their students, descriptors which characterise levels of performance characteristic of first, upper second, lower second, and third classes. This might take the form of a template setting out assessment criteria, and an example of such a template is annexed to this document.

Where different modes of assessment privilege different qualities (for example essay writing in examination conditions, extended essays, dissertations, oral competence) different templates may need to be produced. Such templates or their equivalent should be published in student handbooks. Given that the qualities of the graduate historian will differ from those who have pursued honours degrees in different disciplines, procedures for assessing performance may be different in history from those appropriate to other disciplines.

History departments, sections, or subject groups should have the autonomy to establish criteria for classification appropriate to the discipline and to this benchmark statement. Benchmark standards should inform, but not unduly circumscribe, the approach to determining modes of assessment, and the precise weightings given to assessing different historical skills, methodologies, and learning outcomes.

Published criteria should be available for all forms of assessment, including the assessment of long essays, dissertations, oral presentations, and vivas where any or all of these modes of assessment are used. Criteria at all levels of classification should give predominance to positive achievement, although below the first class they should also indicate the kinds of limitations which disqualify a candidate from achieving a mark in a higher class. Individual institutions might wish to develop new methods for describing undergraduate achievement. The basic threshold for achievement of Honours (H4) must remain the standard required to achieve a Third Class in traditional systems of classification. Describing performance above this level might be done through issuing transcripts rather than by classification.

Institutions might issue transcripts containing assessment marks for all courses or modules and an overall percentage mark (which might be weighted). Such a procedure would discriminate more precisely between different candidates' performance and would enable Institutions to show how a student performed across a range of assessments. Outstanding performance might be rewarded by graduating with distinction. Such a candidate would have achieved the same overall standard as a student graduating first class in a traditional system of classification. An honours degree in History should normally reflect at least two years (or four semesters) of work beyond a previously qualifying standard.

The qualifying standard would normally be one year's study at or equivalent to H1. All graduates in history should demonstrate competence in the discipline and the purpose of schemes of assessment is to evaluate the level of competence achieved. In establishing and maintaining history degree programmes, departments should take into account the following summary of learning outcomes. They will not necessarily wish to include assessment of all these learning outcomes in degree classification:

i. command of a substantial body of historical knowledge;

ii. the ability to develop and sustain historical arguments in a variety of literary forms, formulating appropriate questions and utilising evidence;

iii. an ability to read, analyse, and reflect critically and contextually upon historical texts;

iv. an appreciation of the complexity of reconstructing the past, the problematic and varied nature of historical evidence;

v. an understanding of the varieties of approaches to understanding, constructing, and interpreting the past; and, where relevant, a knowledge of concepts and theories derived from the humanities and social sciences;

vi. the ability to read, analyse, and reflect critically and contextually upon historical texts and other source materials;

vii. the ability to gather and deploy evidence and data to find, retrieve, sort and exchange new information;

viii. a command of comparative perspectives, which may include the ability to compare the histories of different countries, societies, or cultures;

ix. awareness of continuity and change over extended time spans;

x. an understanding of the development of history as a discipline and the awareness of different historical methodologies;

xi. an ability to design, research, and present a sustained and independently-conceived piece of historical writing;

xii. the ability to address historical problems in depth, involving the use of contemporary sources and advanced secondary literature;

xiii. clarity, fluency, and coherence in written expression;

xiv. clarity, fluency, and coherence in oral expression;

xv. the ability to work collaboratively and to participate in group discussion;

xvi. competence in specialist skills which are necessary for some areas of historical analysis and understanding, as appropriate.

5

Teacher Training in Environmental Education

Environmental education is concerned with knowledge, values, and attitudes, and has as its aim responsible environmental behaviour. The link between environmental challenges and human health is a major cause for public concern about the environment. Lead poisoning in paint and pipes, air pollution, pesticides in water and food supplies, increased threats of skin cancer from depletion of the ozone layer, and related environmental challenges are of growing concern to an increasing number of Americans. The public is especially concerned about the effects of these problems on their children and future generations.

Environmental education helps prevent or mitigate environmental human health problems by providing the public with information on how individual and collective actions lead to environmental pollution, how pollutants may affect one's health, how to assess real versus exaggerated environmental health risks, and how to make informed and responsible decisions that prevent or mitigate the effects of pollution on one's health. Educators and public officials generally believe that significant improvements are needed in the nation's public education system to enhance student learning.

Many educational scholars and practitioners agree that "... our students are not doing well at thinking, reasoning, analysing, predicting, estimating, or problem solving...". Many goals of the education reform movement emphasise the importance of strengthening core subjects such as math, science, and geography as well as teaching in an interdisciplinary manner across subject areas. Education reformers are also looking for ways to improve student learning through greater use and development of critical-thinking and problem-solving skills. Finally, many reformers emphasise the importance of relating learning in the classroom to the needs and issues of the community. Environmental education has tremendous potential for contributing to the goals of the education reform movement.

For example, environmental education provides an opportunity to strengthen teaching in many core subjects, especially science, because it is the basis for solving many of our environmental challenges. Environmental education also provides an opportunity to strengthen interdisciplinary teaching because environmental topics can be addressed from many different perspectives, including scientific, historical, cultural, and political perspectives. Finally, environmental education can provide an important opportunity for teachers to bring actual local environmental challenges into the classroom for discussion and problem-solving.

Protecting the environment has the added value of creating new jobs for Americans. Employment opportunities cover the spectrum of careers, from manual labour to high technology and management. For example, there is an increasing demand for individuals with specialised scientific and technical skills to develop more effective environmental pollution prevention and control technologies. There is also a growing demand for trained workers in environmentally related fields. Projected revenues show consistent growth for environmental industries such as air pollution control, environmental energy sources, hazardous waste management, resource recovery, and instrument manufacturing. The Environmental Business Journal reports a composite annual growth rate of 6 percent for these industries. This growth is also reflected in employment forecasts into the next century.

Environmental education and training can help ensure an adequate supply of well-trained environmental personnel to deal with the nation's increasingly complex environmental challenges. Environmental education also improves the quality of the general work force. Environmental education's emphasis on critical thinking and problem-solving better equips students to deal with rapidly changing technologies in the workplace. And environmental education opens new opportunities as the United States exports its environmental skills and technologies to other nations. The future health and welfare of Americans depends on their ability to use the Earth's resources sustainably.

The United Nations World Commission on Environment and Development defines sustainable development as "development that meets the needs of the present without compromising the ability of future generations to meet their own needs." It is critical that we provide future generations of Americans with the same abilities and opportunities that current and past generations have had. In 1992, international leaders came together in Rio de Janeiro to participate in the United Nations Conference on Environment and Development (UNCED). The product of UNCED, Agenda 21, provides guidance to countries so they can meet their own environmental and development goals.

The U.S. response to Agenda 21 is the President's Council on Sustainable Development (PCSD). The PCSD report, Sustainable America: A New Consensus for Prosperity, Opportunity, and a Healthy Environment for the Future, is a series of policy recommendations which will help the U.S. achieve national environmental, economic, and social goals. Like Chapter 36 in Agenda 21, Chapter 3 in Sustainable America focuses on the role of education in sustainability. The recommendations and actions in Chapter 3 have been supplemented with initiatives in another document titled *Education for Sustainability: An Agenda for Action*. Together these reports highlight the important role of education in ensuring a sustainable future.

Sustainable development poses two fundamental education challenges: one is to promote positive attitudes and informed decisions of citizens and government leaders that are conducive to sustainability. The other is to teach people at all levels the benefits of integrating conservation priorities with the need for development. Environmental education has the potential to make a major contribution to sustainable development by demonstrating ways to overcome these two challenges.

First, environmental education research has identified key strategies for developing education programmes that lead to responsible decision-making and action. Second, environmental education practitioners have developed programme models for incorporating a range of perspectives into the resolution of issues. These tools and strategies, developed over decades by environmental educators and field tested on a range of issues where conflicts exist between different interest groups, can be applied immediately to sustainable development.

Interest in protecting natural heritage arises from the respect that most people hold for their nation's past and a belief in its future. It also stems from a desire to protect their natural areas and scenic landscapes, to enjoy them, and to pass them on to their children. Natural heritage also includes the multitude of plant and animal species that inhabit their country. State and privately funded efforts to protect and manage species and their habitats reflect Americans' love for wildlife. Yet many citizens do not understand the ecological and economic importance of preserving biological diversity and that species can be strong indicators of the health of the environment.

Environmental education enhances the public's understanding of the need for biodiversity. Environmental education also educates the public about how their actions affect natural ecosystems and how positive steps taken to minimise impacts on these ecosystems will translate into improvements in overall environment.

Environmental education is taking place across the country-in classrooms and board rooms, in living rooms and urban education centres, in city halls and congressional chambers. How is it being done and who is doing it? What obstacles must we overcome to ensure that all citizens have the knowledge, skills, and attitudes to make informed decisions about the environment? What do professionals face in trying to create an environmentally literate citizenry? Since 1970, a variety of educational institutions, environmental organisations, and government agencies have supported the development, delivery, and evaluation of environmental education in the United States. These environmental education efforts have targeted a variety of audiences, including teachers and students in elementary and secondary education, administrators at all levels, college and university teachers and students, adults and the general public, senior citizens, multi-ethnic communities, and political and business leaders. In general, current environmental education efforts generally fit into one of two sectors:

- Formal environmental education, which consists of activities taking place in elementary and secondary schools, colleges, universities, and technical institutions.
- Nonformal environmental education, which includes activities taking place in businesses, nonprofit organisations, and other institutions that are not considered part of the formal education system, also encompasses activities that involve the media, including newspapers, magazines, television, and computer networks

Within each of these broad sectors, there are several sub-sectors that encompass the majority of environmental education activities taking place today. Collaboration between formal and nonformal sectors is common and widespread, from local nature centres working with school systems to government agencies working with businesses and universities. Such collaboration is essential and it increases the reach and impact of environmental education programmes. Following are the guidelines for environmental education:

- Considers the environment in its totality
- Is a continuous lifelong process
- Embraces interdisciplinary education
- Examines major environmental issues from local, regional, national, and international points of view

- Focuses on current and potential environmental situations, remembering historical perspectives
- Promotes the value and necessity of local, national, and international cooperation
- Explicitly considers environmental aspects in plans for development and growth
- Acknowledges that learners have a role in planning learning and an opportunity for making decisions and accepting their consequences
- Emphasises environmental sensitivity, knowledge, problem-solving skills, and values clarification at every age
- Helps learners discover the symptoms and real causes of environmental challenges
- Emphasises the complexity of problems

Formal Environmental Education Efforts

Formal environmental education efforts focus on developing awareness, knowledge, skills, and motivation in students, teachers, and school administrators. Activities involve curriculum development; teacher and administrator training initiatives; local, state, and national school reform activities; evaluation; the development of national environmental education guidelines; and other related programmes designed to improve elementary, secondary, and post-secondary education. It divides the formal sector into activities for grades kindergarten through 12 (K-12) and post-secondary education activities. However, there is overlap between the two, especially in regard to teacher training and curriculum development.

Delivery of environmental education programmes in K-12 education generally takes two approaches, with many school systems adopting some combination of the two. The most prevalent trend in elementary and secondary education is toward an approach called "infusion." This approach integrates environmental education into existing lessons, units, or topics focusing on other subjects such as history, science, and the social sciences. For example, students may learn how to solve a local environmental challenge-such as chemical contamination of a nearby stream-using scientific methods that include testing, identifying, and locating the source of contamination. Students may also learn how to solve this contamination problem by exploring historical dimensions for how this type of problem has been addressed in other communities, how governmental agencies can help, and how citizens can get involved.

Ideally, infusion results in the incorporation of environmental education-an inherently interdisciplinary field-into all aspects of the curriculum at every grade level. Infusion recognises that environmental issues cut across disciplinary lines, and that environmental responsibility relies on knowledge, skills, and attitudes that incorporate, but also go beyond, basic scientific understanding. Because no one asks schools to do less-in fact, many demand they do more-infusion is a pragmatic approach to ensuring that environmental education can be incorporated into a crowded curriculum. But despite the arguments in favour of infusion, many environmental educators are wary. Their concern is that environmental education may be short-changed or ignored unless it receives its own place in the curriculum.

For this reason, many educators prefer the "second-course" or "block" approach. This approach consists of offering separate and distinct "environmental" courses. Their argument is that the separate course approach can offer depth that is missing in the infusion approach, as well as an identifiable focus for attracting funding, evaluating progress, and encouraging career development. According to recent data, most states rely on infusion as the main approach for integrating environmental education into the curriculum. However, more distinct environmental courses are being offered in middle and secondary schools, and many educators believe that this trend will continue.

In addition, more schools are offering current events classes that include an environmental focus. At the college and university level, environmental education is addressed in a variety of ways; however, the effectiveness of these efforts varies from state to state, institution to institution, and course to course, just as it does at the K-12 level. Courses and programmes are offered that prepare students for specific environmental careers, including environmental science, natural resource management, environmental design, environmental engineering, environmental planning, and environmental management.

Many universities and colleges also offer degrees in environmental studies, which differ from more technical programmes in that they are interdisciplinary and include both the natural sciences (such as biology, resource management, Environmental Education in the Schools In 1995, three states had mandates requiring environmental education training for teachers. In addition, eleven states required environmental education to be incorporated into core curricula and biochemistry) and the social sciences. A relatively small number of universities and colleges offer undergraduate and graduate degrees in environmental education, which are designed to train students for careers as professional environmental educators working in formal and nonformal settings.

Some areas have very limited opportunities for student teachers to receive training in environmental education before they enter the classroom. On the other hand, some states, such as Wisconsin, have mandates requiring nearly all students training to become teachers to achieve environmental education competencies before being licensed to teach. In some institutions, students can take a specific environmental education or environmental studies course. In others, they receive environmental education content and methodologies through other courses-often in science or general methodology classes.

Unfortunately, most environmental education training for teachers takes place after they leave the university and start teaching-as a result of in-service training or individual teacher initiative. There is a growing trend among universities to include environmental education requirements for all students-not just those majoring in environmentally related fields. For example, Tufts University initiated an Environmental Literacy Institute for university professors from around the world to help them incorporate environmental education into all coursework, from creative writing to politics to law. This programme was initiated in 1993 and has involved more than 150 universities and organisations from around the world.

In addition, more than 250 universities and organisations have become signatories to the Talloires Declaration, which supports an interdisciplinary approach to environmental literacy at the university level. Another trend is the emergence of environmental management education in business schools across the country. Several business schools are currently incorporating environmental content into their curriculum, hoping to influence the attitudes and behaviour of current and future business graduates regarding the link between a healthy economy and a healthy environment. Universities and colleges have taken the lead in conducting a broad spectrum of environmental education research projects concerning environmental knowledge, skills, attitudes, and action.

Findings have been published in a variety of periodicals, such as The Journal of Environmental Education and in conference proceedings and monographs such as those produced by the North American Association for Environmental Education (NAAEE). Through NAAEE's North American Commission on Environmental Education Research, faculty from nearly 20 universities, including Rutgers University, Ohio State University, the University of Wisconsin-Stevens Point, and Northern Illinois University, have cooperated in identifying and addressing research needs in environmental education. Community and technical colleges have become increasingly active in providing training programmes in the environmental field, offering specific degree programmes for such careers as water/wastewater technicians and course offerings on a variety of specific topics.

At present, these programmes focus mainly on technical aspects of job performance and regulatory compliance, but the opportunity exists for a broader environmental education approach that also encompasses the nature of the environmental challenges that prompted the need for regulation. Community colleges, in particular, provide a substantial resource for minority students, many of which graduate and attend universities for advanced degrees. A variety of environmental education activities taking place in the formal sector involve collaboration between university and college programmes and the nation's elementary and secondary schools. They also involve collaboration with nonformal institutions, government agencies, and other institutions.

For example, many universities and colleges are involved in developing environmental education curriculum for K-12, enhancing in-service training, and evaluating environmental education curriculum materials and training. And many nonprofit organisations, such as environmental organisations and community educational institutions, are involved in training teachers, developing supplementary environmental education materials, and conducting programmes for parents, families, youth, and the public.

Nonformal Environmental Education Programmes

Nonformal environmental education activities take place in a variety of settings throughout the country-from zoos, museums, aquariums, nature centres, and science centres to parks, and community centres. Nonformal environmental education programmes often complement and enhance formal education programmes. In addition, many target adults, the general public, or families. And some are designed for specific adult audiences, such as senior citizens, public policy makers, business leaders, and women's groups.

The goals of nonformal environmental education programmes are similar to those in the formal sector-developing environmentally literate young people and adults who have the knowledge, skills, and motivation to make informed decisions about the environment. Activities in this sector involve community action projects sponsored by business and nonformal education organisations; programmes in local, state, and national parks, wildlife refuges, and other natural areas; television, radio, and other media programmes focused on environmental issues and actions; and a variety of partnership programmes designed to improve elementary, secondary, and post-secondary education. In many cases, nonformal environmental education activities are directed toward the solution of specific environmental challenges. It should be recognised that in reaching adults, there is a potentially strong link between formal and nonformal education.

Parents' awareness and understanding of environmental issues are frequently enhanced by their children's involvement in environmental education. As children become involved in the problem solving and action elements of effective environmental education, they frequently take these issues home and involve their parents in discussions about them. One of the central challenges to nonformal environmental education is how best to reach a non-captive, out-of-school audience with a meaningful and effective programme. What kind of education programme will prompt behaviour change or commitment to get involved in local, national, and global environmental issues? To address this problem, environmental education efforts in the nonformal sector vary widely.

Newspapers, magazines, television, movies, and other media can transmit messages to large audiences, and have been gaining popularity as a means for educating the public about environmental issues. There are many excellent examples of media-based environmental education, such as attempts to educate about recycling; however, media efforts face two major challenges. The first is assuring that environmental messages publicised as education really are education rather than hype or propaganda. The second challenge is assuring breadth and depth in examining complex environmental issues.

Entertainment and the media often emphasise environmental awareness, rather than education that leads to personal, organisational, or community participation. Many nonformal institutions are involved in programmes and activities that target specific audiences such as senior citizens, culturally diverse students and adults, preschoolers, tourists, policy makers, and most often, the general public. In some communities, schools, businesses, and nonformal institutions collaborate to reach a specific target audience. Many community institutions offer continuing education programmes for adults and families focusing on environmental topics, as well as after-school, summer, and weekend environmental education programmes for young people.

In addition, some churches, synagogues, and other religious institutions are involved in environmental education activities that link religion with environmental stewardship. Many organisations and institutions, from government agencies to environmental nonprofit organisations and businesses, have developed supplementary environmental education materials that are used in schools and community settings. These materials include a wide range of topics and approaches, from those dealing with a single subject such as solid waste to those focusing on broad environmental themes such as sustainable development. Some are meant to supplement formal school curricula. Others are meant to be used with students and adults in nonformal settings. The quality of these supplementary materials varies greatly.

Many K-12 educators receive environmental education training as a result of in-service training that takes place after they begin teaching. Much of this training takes place through workshops at national, regional, or state environmental education conferences, or courses sponsored by local university outreach and extension programmes, often in conjunction with nonformal partners, such as museums, zoos, or science centres. Many teachers also participate in specialised workshops, such as those offered by Project Learning Tree, World Resources Institute, World Wildlife Fund, and other nonprofit educational organisations. These courses and workshops often provide "continuing education units" or specific college credits that many teachers need to maintain certification to teach.

Infants first learn about their world through touch. When we share our joys with our children, there is an inherent feeling response. Touch an infant's cheek, and she will turn towards the touch. Put your finger by her hand, and she will hold onto it. Take a toddler for a walk, stop and show intense interest in a banana slug, and it is likely that the child will be curious too. It is an easy thing to take children outdoors. It also seems like a good thing to many parents, especially if their children are young, and so it is not difficult to "sell" the value of the experience. As our young ones grow up, however, their days become loaded with other valuable endeavours we have created for them: six and a half hours at school, time for after-school sports, music, friends, and then homework, chores, family time for the fortunate ones; bedtime comes all too soon.

The value we placed on outdoor exploration when they were very young is replaced by an overabundance of extracurricular activities. It seems a very difficult undertaking for most of us to get our children into the wilderness or even to a local natural area. Stewardship of our environment follows an interest in and understanding of the natural world. If a child spends most of each day indoors, what is that experience to beget but an understanding and interest in our indoor culture? This relationship is nurtured through repeated experiences and develops alongside greater familiarity with a species. For this interest and curiosity to be fully realised, one must purposefully experience the out-of-doors. Several excursions with a toddler is a great beginning, but we need to continue to help the child hold that sense of wonder in later years.

To develop understanding, and further stewardship, experiences need to be repeated or offered many times. Eventually, several characteristics of a slug may become quite familiar to the child and subsequent forays into a natural setting should be a personal adventure - not a homework assignment. With several visits to the same spot, children begin to notice more of the area's biodiversity. Environmental education needs to be open to changing the way they do business, and that means recognising the wider connections between environmental concerns and social and economic justice.

It also means celebrating diversity at all levels in the field of environmental education. There is simply a lack of representation of people of colour and their perspectives. In a recent conversation with an environmental justice leader in our community, she said that "environmental education must tell the truth about what white culture has done to the environment and why. This response demonstrates a well-founded suspicion of white motives, and is representative of a widespread feeling of resentment among people of colour who don't think that white people have the right to claim ownership of the environmental movement when they have not taken ownership of the problems.

Environmental education often fails to address issues in such a way that it is clear where the problems originate. This kind of clarity would mean being honest about the history of industrial capitalism, colonial exploitation, the institutionalisation of poverty, and intentional disenfranchisement of people of colour. This way of looking at the issues might be uncomfortable for many white people, which is one reason these issues are not prominent on the agenda of mainstream environmental education in the United States. The same goes for environmental education. For an environmental education organisation's work to be relevant, for it to have a lasting value, it has to connect with the lives of children and point to ways that they can make a difference. This means first identifying the problems around us, many of which are invisible.

Environmental education needs to embrace issues that are totally relevant and are a high priority in the local community and to the broadest possible range of people and make them a part of our everyday curriculum. This means being inclusive of people of colour and considering global justice issues in curriculum writing and decision-making for environmental education. Organisations must commit to anti-racism and anti-poverty and commit to the addressing the issues that are of greatest importance to those they seek to serve. We now know that diversity is critical to a strong, healthy environment.

As environmental educators, we know that diverse ecosystems are healthier, creating a powerful synergy not available to monoculture systems. This same concept of diversity should apply to the communities where we live, the organisations we are part of, and the teaching that we do. Developing the naturalist intelligence is no different than teaching math or reading skills. Teachers must provide the opportunity for this intelligence to grow. We need to stop and consider the implications this identified intelligence has on our educational settings.

Getting on a bus and moving to an appropriate expedition site extends learning beyond walking down the hall to the gym or the art room. Doing field studies extends experiential learning beyond working with pattern blocks in math class. By observing outside we can see those same patterns in nature and understand connections. Employable success in the future requires that our children be computer literate. We have stocked our classrooms and constructed computer labs to provide this opportunity. The quality of life on this planet requires that our children have experience with nature. We must provide the best educational learning opportunities for the Naturalist Intelligence.

All teachers are facing reforms that include state essential learnings and national standards. Naturalist topics and themes make some of the best curriculum integrations that will help us reach these goals. An example would be the themes of change, cycles, and connections. Teachers in the Pacific Northwest could establish integrated studies around marine ecology, watersheds, forests, aquatic life. The instructors in the Southwest could focus on the desert environment. After all, intelligence has been defined as solving problems and fashioning products valued in one culture or community. Knowing and understanding your community environment and using it as an extended classroom just makes sense.

One simple way to encourage the Naturalist Intelligence is to take students outside to explore their school community. Careful observation will find weeds in the cracks of almost any playground surface. The eaves of a roof provide nesting places for birds. Water from storm runoff pours down storm drains in the parking lot. A teacher's primary responsibility is to be sure all children experience success and learn. We must consider each child and provide the skills they need to grow. We must consider all ways to deliver curriculum.

For the elementary teacher, teaching for the Naturalist Intelligence provides the key to integration. All levels of students need these types of experiences. Our generation grew up riding our bikes to the nearest park or vacant lot to play and explore. Children today are not permitted this freedom. They are more easily supervised and are safer at home in front of the TV. Teachers should provide opportunities that encourage:

- sensory observation: feeling, smelling, listening
- data collection from observation
- grouping of natural objects (classification)
- observation of animal behaviour
- growing things...plants, garden, butterfly garden
- recycling projects and worm boxes
- field studies...out of doors
- observation through the microscope, telescope, binoculars, hand lens
- drawing, sketching, photographing, video taping nature
- manipulating outdoor equipment or kits (water testing kits or nets)
- outdoor silent observation, reflection, journaling
- identifying sounds in nature
- interacting with animals (bugs) and plants

- establishment of a nature trail, viewing deck, or outdoor classroom,
- making scientific instruments (inventing)
- designing experiments
- field trips (real, electronic, video, guided imagery)
- walks outside for fresh air, sounds of nature, and dirt underfoot
- modelling, measurement, or scale drawings of animals, plants, or outdoor settings
- writing poems or songs using adjectives from the outdoors
- identifying shapes in natural setting
- observation of plants or out of doors change over the course of the school year
- observing a fruit, vegetable or other plant or animal material decompose overtime
- collecting trash or other items (rocks, feathers, flowers, leaves...) in the school yard and group (classify) the items by their characteristics (shape, colour, etc.)
- read aloud stories/articles relating to the out of doors, space, natural phenomena, animals, or plants
- performing role plays of cycles in nature, animal behaviour, plant growth etc.

Environmental Education Materials

Environmental Education (EE) materials should foster awareness of the natural and build environment, an understanding of environmental concepts, conditions, and issues, and an awareness of the feelings, values, attitudes, and perceptions at the heart of environmental issues, as appropriate for different developmental levels. These materials should build lifelong skills that enable learners to prevent and address environmental issues and promote civic responsibility, encouraging learners to use their knowledge, personal skills, and assessments of environmental issues as a basis for environmental problem solving and action. EE materials should rely on instructional techniques that create an effective learning environment and should be well designed and easy to use.

Environmental education creates opportunities where students can have a direct experience with what is, for many of them, a separate reality. It is implied that through the process of environmental education students will develop knowledge about and concern for the natural world. The task of the instructor is to craft appropriate experiences in reflection of both "place" and "learner." These students from Brooklyn did not need a lecture on forest ecology, nor did they require expensive scientific equipment. All they needed was to be in the woods. Environmental education in the United States has developed along a bifurcated path.

On one hand, we think of environmental education as strategies emphasising the development of scientific knowledge and technical or managerial solutions to environmental problems. However, there is also the dimension of environmental studies that seeks to instill a sense of caring and responsibility for the earth. The synergism of these goals fuels both the enthusiasm for and the confusion about defining environmental education. The opportunities have never been greater, nor the need more urgent, for an environmental education. Environmental education did not spring forth fully formed from any one discipline, but rather as a product of a co-evolutionary process within science, public awareness of environmental issues, and educational ideas.

Environmental thought in the United States has its roots in the Romantic-Nature Movement of the late 19th and early 20th centuries. Then, the difficult lessons of the dust bowl era in the 1930's and the extinction of previously abundant species such as the passenger pigeon sobered Americans into the development of the Conservation Movement, an approach to science that merged environmental thinking, science and life practice. Aldo Leopold, a college professor from Wisconsin, became the primary spokesman for the conservation movement. In the 1960's, Rachel Carson's Silent Spring led to the first Earth Day celebration in 1970.

In that same year, President Nixon signed into law Title Three, which provided funding for and mandated that every state develop and incorporate environmental education strategies and curriculum into their schools. Many schools in the early 1970's returned to Sharp's school camping model in order to fulfil their federal environmental education mandate. Federal financial support then sparked an explosion of summer camps adapting their facilities to serve school groups throughout the year. Despite the disintegration of federal dollars in the late 1970's, residential environmental education continues to be one of the most popular expressions of experiential and environmental education available to school districts. Today these programmes are largely funded by the school districts themselves or by parents.

The events surrounding the twentieth anniversary of the first Earth Day coupled with the 1992 United Nations Earth Summit renewed Americans' interest in the environment and its potential role in education. However, as environmental education became an increasingly mainstream educational practice, it has become the subject of heightened analysis and tension. There are basically two areas of contention. One relates to the ongoing debate of accuracy and fairness in environmental education materials and methods that has been historically fueled by industry. The second relates to environmental education's potential role in the educational reform movement. During the last decade in particular, there has been considerable debate regarding the political motivations of environmental curricula. These arguments seem to coincide with the movement towards conservatism in the United States.

In response to these concerns, in 1997, the Independent Commission on Environmental Education reviewed nearly 80 national and regional environmental education curricula for their accuracy in presenting environmental science and problems. Their work revealed that most materials presented environmental science accurately reflecting current and evolving thought. However, some materials contained either consistent factual inaccuracies or misstated theories of science. Concurrent to the work of the Independent Commission on Environmental Education, the North American Association for Environmental Education (NAAEE) developed their own guidelines for professional practice and programme development. The NAAEE guidelines specifically address issues of fairness and accuracy in the development of environmental education materials, student assessment and literacy as well as professional teacher development.

However, the guidelines are entirely voluntary, providing no requirements for compulsory adoption. Environmental education also has contributed to the ongoing national debate on educational reform. The State

Education and Environment Roundtable has advanced project-based interdisciplinary studies as a way of breaking down the traditional compartmentalised approach to education. Identified as using the Environment as an Integrating Context for learning, their guidelines incorporate the following goals:

1. Break down the traditional boundaries between disciplines.
2. Provide hands-on learning experiences through problem-solving and project-based activities.
3. Create collaborative relationships between teachers.
4. Adapt to individual students and their unique skills and abilities.
5. Develop knowledge, understanding and appreciation for the environment, community and natural surroundings.

The works of the NAAEE and SEER are focused on defining a new or clearer path for environmental education. There is also an emerging field of environmental education research that is attempting to identify the significant life experiences of pro-environmental adults and how those events have shaped their life choices. Despite the ongoing difficulties in securing funding for environmental education projects and the inherent challenges of teaching the dynamic subject of environmental studies, the future prospects for environmental education are both bright and urgent.

The task of preparing youth for an ever-changing world will require the constant evaluation and revision of our educational programmes and methodology. As reflective environmental educators, we must consider tools that will help us be more effective in our practice without straying from the foundational strengths of the movement. Toward that end, schools and educational organisations must strive to select the methodological pathways and curricular tools that will meet the needs of their students both present and future. Environmental education centres must challenge themselves to adopt institutional practices that model the same sorts of ideals they present in their educational programmes – to do less is to suggest hypocrisy. This involves committing to sustainability in design and practice, thus embodying what Oberlin College professor David Orr has referred to as a "crystallised pedagogy," or to put it more simply, to practice what you preach. It also involves research: educational research for the growth of the environmental education profession and scientific research for the furtherance of knowledge and for the children's exposure to genuine science.

Effective environmental education brings about an increased awareness and appreciation of nature. It also reveals, in context, the wounds or separations that exist between the human and nonhuman worlds. Therefore, the problem every environmental educator must address is how to motivate students into action without terrifying them into inaction. Environmental educators that fail to address the potential fear-producing effect of their lessons risk creating in their students a calloused or even fearful attitude toward nature, what educator David Sobel has referred to as "Ecophobia." Australian educator Noel Gough has commented that environmental educators need to provide students with more complex and complicated discourse.

The inevitability of earth transformation does not preclude us from mindful decisions regarding the appropriateness of our actions. To be aware of the world around us is not enough, nor is it enough to be knowledgeable of ecology and earth systems. The critically important relationships we have with the natural world, including clean air, potable water and fertile soil, require the thoughtful application of personal and social practice. Creatively exercised, environmental education provides the context of concern necessary to develop this thoughtful application. As environmental educators, we are teaching in the present, preparing students for the future. We must strive to create educational experiences that challenge our students' perspectives both locally and globally. Whether we use a field guide or a database, the strength of our curricular tools is measured through the life actions of our students.

Teaching Strategies

The interlacing fields of outdoor, adventure, and environmental education are not easily distinguished. One strand that links these three fields is the emphasis on experiential learning. Improved interpersonal skills and learner empowerment are often primary intended outcomes. What are these three aspects of education? Even outdoor, environmental, and adventure education practitioners struggle to distinguish among them, if they bother to try at all. In Effective Leadership in Adventure Programming, Simon Priest and Mike Gass explain that genuine experiential education involves "learning by doing with reflection,".

Outdoor education follows the experiential philosophy of learning by doing. It takes place primarily, but not exclusively, through involvement with the natural environment. In outdoor education, the emphasis for a subject of learning is placed on relationships concerning people and natural resources. Priest and Gass claim that historically, adventure education and environmental education have been identified as two branches of outdoor education: adventure education emphasising intra- and inter-personal relationships, while environmental education emphasises ecological principles and ekistic relationships.

Environmental education is far broader than a branch of outdoor education, occurring both indoors and outdoors, in both formal and non formal settings, and growing out of the conservation movement as much as from outdoor education. Environmental education plays a seminal role in many outdoor education programmes, including playing an increasing part in adventure-based programmes. The three fields —outdoor, adventure and environmental education —would fit more appropriately in a Venn diagram of intertwined circles, with overlap and individuality for each.

Considerations of place are growing in many educational environments. Primary school teachers are told that children should learn first about the amazing animals in their own part of the world before studying dinosaurs and tropical rainforests. Service learning emphasises bringing students into the communities in which they live. Adventure education emphasises the value of taking people into new and strange worlds. Places play two critical yet distinct roles in laying the backdrop for successful education. The first is helping learners to connect with home and community. The second is challenging learners to see the world with new eyes, by exposing them to strange new worlds. With the advent of modern society, place got lost in the compartmentalisation and institutionalisation of education.

Looking back to how people learned before education was separated from everyday life, landscapes taught children about geography; plant and animal life taught them math and science skills; by sustaining the people, this inspired the development of skills needed for survival and creativity; and stories from the land taught children communication skills as well as about their culture and morals. With the expansion of human knowledge came the impossibility of knowing everything, and thus the compartmentalising of knowledge. Within our current urban society, survival skills sometimes involve computing sums or writing reports, instead of finding shelter and gathering food.

The arts offer more varied media, and more sources for inspiration. These changes were both bad and good, and now many wise people are reflecting on the value of regaining some of what we lost: the sense of community, integrated learning, and education with apparent practical application for the learner. Place-based education is one way of bringing some of that holistic, active learning back into the child's life experience. This demonstrates a connection between the classroom and the child's world outside of academia. This does not mean that tropical rainforests and dinosaurs should not be taught in the classroom.

Children are passionate about these captivating worlds! It simply means that children will also be fascinated by their own nearby worlds, if they are given the opportunity to discover them, and learn about them. This includes the urban homes of many children, as well as the nearby wilder places that require a school bus to see. It includes the people of their home communities and the experience of how their water, food and clothes arrive in their neighbourhoods, and where it all goes when we throw it away. And, as people develop a sense of place within their own communities, we can also offer them the thrill of discovering new and different worlds... and making the connection between their experiences in strange places with their lives closer to home. Outdoor, experiential, environmental, and adventure educators have known for generations that place can have a significant impact on student learning.

In the 1950's, school camping was viewed as an excellent setting in which to build citizenship among the nation's youth. Since then, residential experiences for school children, Outward Bound-style adventure programmes, and the field of wilderness therapy have surged in number and quality, both in the United States and in many other parts of the world. When places are actively sensed, the physical landscape becomes wedded to the landscape of the mind, to the roving imagination, and where the mind may lead is anybody's guess. Considerations of place are surging again in many progressive environments. Among adventure leaders, many have experienced the impact of learning in unusual, wild, or beautiful places—and thus become advocates of the wilderness experience.

Having taught in natural settings from the coast to mountain peaks, many students, inspired by a place, stop and contemplate the significance of what they are doing and learning. Facilitating student reflection on their experience means providing the time and the place, and sometimes the discussion, for them to make connections that they themselves are best able to make. Place-based education is, first and foremost, an effort to help learners to make connections. If we as educators can help our students to feel connected to their homes, their communities, and the natural worlds that surround them, then we will be taking the first step towards a caring citizenry that understands—and thus cares about and for—their places on the planet. Through place-based experiences that inspire and empower, students will become the citizens this planet needs to sustain humanity and ecosystems across the globe.

Technologies in Environmental Education

In a world where we are frequently exposed to controversial high-tech headlines about self replicating miniature robots, attempts to download human brains into computers, and cars with night vision and heads up displays. In a recent survey of environmental centres, Bethany Lesure found the most common reasons for integrating technology into educational programmes are "audience demand", "State Ed. Requirement", a way to "Reach Out", and that "Kids Relate" to technology. Integrating technology into our educational programmes provides students with additional tools to enhance their learning. So you might wonder, "What are the benefits of taking this approach to help students explore and understand the world around them?"

Technology supports our efforts to appeal to different learning styles. With a variety of learning tools, students can understand their experiences through verbal, .written, spatial, quantitative, and/or graphical means. As a result, many more students become engaged in the learning process. Technology supports our multidisciplinary approach to learning. Integrating different disciplines helps students combine their mathematical, logical, scientific, linguistic, artistic, and social knowledge to make their lives and interactions with the world clearer. Technology is integral to modern science.

Modelling the research techniques of biologists, engineers, and other professionals, helps students use technology to measure, document, interpret, obtain, and manage data. Technology aids our efforts in supporting teachers. Regardless of their disciplines, few teachers currently receive training in the use of technology. Technology allows us not only to demonstrate teaching strategies, but also to deliver training, which provides teachers with the skills and confidence to become leaders in their classrooms and schools. Technology gives us a way to connect with each other and extend the learning experience.

Interactive web elements and participation in video conferencing provide students with experiences before their visits to IslandWood, and allows them to continue projects after their stay at our campus. There are many definitions used to define "technology," particularly when looking at how it is used in education. Since we interact with the environment through our senses, using technology seems a logical element of instruction about the environment. The plethora of digital cameras on the market allows to capture all sorts of images that previously have been fleeting.

Simple adapters are available, and even specialised instruments that make it easy to capture and save digital images from microscopes, binoculars and telescopest. In our lab classrooms, we have microscopes hooked up to video screens so children can see what it should look like before they look into their own microscope—a valuable "clue" to provide feedback if you've never used a microscope before.

Similarly, a video screen on a spotting scope in the bird blind helps new users understand how to use their own scopes and binoculars. A great digital camera activity involves kids taking pictures of each other to learn constellations. Each child researches and chooses his or her own constellation. They then pose in a manner similar to the figures associated with constellation and have a buddy take their picture. We can use technology to speed up or slow down time. High speed movies allow us to "slow down" time and see how milk splashes, or how cats lick. Time-lapse photography allows us to see how slow process work.

Handheld devices, Palms and PocketPCs, are a great way to get technology into children's hands at a fairly affordable price. The advantage of these devices is that they run lots of software, so they are multifunctional. We use handheld computers to collect data, help analyse data, and as a multimedia reference. Imagiworks produces ImagiProbe - a sensor-based data acquisition system that enables students to conduct authentic scientific investigations much as research scientists do. We use probes to measure temperature and pH of various bodies of water on our campus as the children study stream health.

CyberTracker is another great tool for the Palm devices. It helps children step through the process of identifying what species they've "seen." We've also created a collection of simple web pages for animals specific to our location to act as a multimedia reference. With this guide installed on a PocketPC, our instructors, and the children, have a field guide that not only shows pictures and words, but can play the vocalisations of birds.

By working through the sounds on the PocketPC or tracks or scat in CyberTracker, children learn that sight is not the only way to make a PID (Positive Identification.) Computers, themselves, have a role in what many people think of when discussing "Technology" in education. They are great ways to find information and learn facts, manipulate that information, and communicate what has been learned.

Spreadsheets are great applications for helping kids display data graphically—if there's only one thing you are allowed to do on a computer with data, have kids learn to create graphs. Students can easily build, test, and evaluate qualitative models without needing to know the underlying calculus driving these models. They can create models that represent their theories about the scientific phenomena studied in class, and they can run simulations in order to test their models. The action of an individual or society that has an impact on other societies constitutes a global issue.

Global climate change, airborne toxins, ozone depletion, and solid waste management are but a few of the global issues that are of current concern for our environment. How do learners and educators know which global issues are important to their lives, and where do they acquire their knowledge and skills to deal with these environmental issues? In a longitudinal study of fifth and ninth graders in Ohio, school classes were found to be increasingly influential in the acquisition of knowledge about the environment. Although students ranked movies and television as the most influential sources of knowledge about specific environmental issues in 1979, by 1983 and 1987 those sources had been replaced by classes in school as being most influential.

High school environmental education courses are often the last formal exposure to environmental issues for non-college-bound students. These courses can be used as valuable opportunities for extending environmental knowledge on global issues and disseminating materials. Such courses can culminate environmental experiences and can clarify and structure knowledge and skills gained from earlier experiences. But learning occurs only when there is meaning in outcomes. Environmental issues, especially global issues, can often appear nebulous and disconnected from a learner's life. Because of the multidisciplinary and interdisciplinary nature of environmental education, it is often difficult to define.

Environmental education can mean concepts in ecology, outdoor education, environmental science or instruction about issues. A primary goal of environmental education, though, is the development of responsible environmental behaviour in citizens, both as individuals and societal groups. The global ramifications of individual or collective action on the rest of the world have only recently become concerns for society. Historic views of air and water were that the abundance and vastness of these resources allowed for unlimited use and abuse.

Today, additional chemical burdens on the environment and alterations of the natural systems have increased. This has been coupled with an increased understanding of the effects of human action on the environment, including long term effects. Every human action has an impact on the environment, both immediately and globally. In a formal education setting, it would seem that incorporating environmental issues into the curriculum would be relatively easy; but experience would suggest otherwise.

Environmental education programmes have been designed for either infusion into existing curricula or the insertion of new courses into study. Framing, a third alternative can be especially effective in learning about global issues. In the infusion approach, content and skills are integrated into existing courses so as to focus on that content without losing the integrity of the courses themselves. For example, an elementary mathematics class might calculate the amount of solid waste that 30 students produce in a year, or the issue of airborne toxins can be used when studying about prevailing winds in an earth science class. Infusion is most often seen in elementary and middle school levels, but less in high school where classes are departmentalised and topically related.

Insertion, the addition of specific courses in environmental education, tends to be used more at the high school level. A course in global issues or environmental issues which is developed on the issues investigation skills format is an example of insertion. Framing moves beyond the arbitrary boundaries of traditional disciplines by creating a framework which allows learning to be related and integrated within a student's life. Using this approach, educators and students can investigate, interpret, explore, manage, discover, and make decisions about global issues.

When studying about global issues, the goal needs to be more than merely acquiring scientific knowledge. A relationship must be made between the individual action and responsibility to the global issue. One approach toward creating an opportunity for meaningful learning is through decision-making and problem-solving approaches with global issues.

Infusion provides teachers with opportunities for drawing upon other disciplines in seeking solution for problems. There are many situations in which creative problem solving dealing with environmental issues can be used in learning settings. Before students can address global environmental issues, they must be knowledgeable about problem identification, interrelationships and alternatives.

During the 1980s, environmental educators used surveys to determine the needs for environmental education programmes. Educators recommended that environmental endeavours focus not only on awareness, but also on attitudes, skill development and citizenship participation in environmental problem solving. A need was indicated by teachers for a new curricula on all academic levels to address the goals on environmental education. Knowledge and awareness of ecological issues were met to a greater extent as higher levels of learning included investigation of issues, evaluation of solutions, and citizenship action.

Environmental issues of global concern are known to students and to educators.

If asked to identify issues, most would be able to identify several: global climate change, ozone depletion, acid rain, deforestation, ocean dumping, and so on. The challenge of environmental education is to make these global issues meaningful to learners by focusing on individual contributions to the problems, and then, using problem-solving, decision-making strategies to develop, refine and redirect the thinking and the learning.

Human survival depends on a number of natural resources. Water is certainly one such resource; air is another; and energy sources such as fossil fuels are a third. Reviewing the presence and effects of pollutants in each of these natural resources is a helpful way to begin a discussion of the role of higher education in preparing future professionals to prevent environmental destruction. Water is a resource with unique properties, essential to all life. It is a basic factor in the growth of natural communities and human civilisations.

The safety of a drinking water supply is influenced by impurities that fall into three classes: organic chemicals, inorganic chemicals, and microorganisms. Discharge of wastewater represents a growing threat to water supplies by adding all three of these impurities to water resources. Wastewater from cities, industries, mining operations, farms, and rural homes contains organic, inorganic, and microorganism impurities that can and do contaminate drinking water supplies. If organic pollutants present in wastewater are not removed, they can rob water of the dissolved oxygen normally present.

Also, organic chemicals such as pesticides may directly poison aquatic organisms, including those connected to human food supplies. Inorganic chemicals in wastewater such as certain phosphorus and nitrogen compounds can cause excessive overgrowth of algae. Microorganisms in discharged wastewater are a major cause of disease. For many years industrial and municipal wastes have been buried in landfills, in abandoned wells and mines, or discharged directly into rivers and other bodies of water. Only recently have we come to better understand how these practices can pollute groundwater, which was once thought to be the safest source for drinking water.

Air is as essential as water; however, numerous pollutants taint the air we breathe. Misuse of fossil fuels has polluted the air so severely that in some regions it is a significant cause of death. Solid particles such as lead, asbestos, and soot are dispersed in the air. Liquid droplets of hydrocarbons and sulphuric acid float in the atmosphere. Gases such as carbon monoxide, nitrogen oxides, and sulphur dioxide are mixed in the atmosphere that surrounds us. These pollutants may impair breathing and exacerbate heart and lung diseases. The landscape is also influenced because forests and other vegetation are sensitive to air pollutants.

Construction materials such as mortar and metal are corroded by some of these pollutants. Smog and acid rain are a few other examples of the effects of air pollution. Energy sources are essential and commonly used in three ways. First, the energy released by mining and burning fossil fuel may be used directly as heat. Second, the heat energy might be converted into work, using refined oil to run machinery and power automobiles. Third, the heat energy from either fossil fuel or nuclear sources may be converted to electricity. All of these uses of energy discharge pollution in forms that can range from waste heat to radioactive materials.

The last few decades have seen a strong movement begin to clean the environment from these pollutants released by new technologies and lack of concern for their effects. This lack of concern may be due to the dearth of understanding by engineers of the effects of these technologies on the environment, and also to a preference for economic factors over ethical factors. Nonetheless, cleanup costs may be shown to be many times greater than the cost of educating engineers to protect the environment and to build in them strong ethical behaviour to protect natural resources. The average cost to clean a contaminated groundwater site under the U.S. Superfund cleanup programme, for example, is $25 million.

Cleaning up some polluted sites is even more expensive than this average. For example, cleaning up lead-contaminated soil and groundwater from an eastern U.S. site where automobile batteries were discarded will cost an estimated $40 million. And the cleanup cost of toxic metal and acid releases from California's Iron Mountain Mine is estimated to approach $1 billion. Thousands of such polluted sites can be found worldwide, and estimating the cost to clean up all of these sites is likely to yield a staggering number. In the U.S. alone, estimates place the total cost of cleaning up all the private and public polluted sites as high as $500 billion to $1 trillion.

In addition to paying for cleanup, the high cost of pollution is often incurred in terms of human health. Some human costs are local. For example, in the Great Lakes region of the U.S. and Canada, children born to women who have high levels of PCBs (polychlorinated biphenyls) from widespread improper disposal suffer retarded growth and score significantly lower on certain memory tests. Other human costs are global. In 2002, the World Health

Organisation listed unsafe water as one of the top ten health risks worldwide.

Widely-read publications indicate that an estimated 1 billion people worldwide drink contaminated water. Also worldwide, urban air pollution killed an estimated 800,000 people in 2002. Lead pollution killed an estimated 234,000 people. These few examples illustrate the high cost of pollution, both in terms of the money required for cleanup and in terms of the impact on human health. The cost of pollution is many times greater than the cost of educating engineers to protect the environment and its natural resources.

Environment Education for Adults

Environmental problems occupy a primary place in adult education. They concern the natural environment of communities, which cannot be understood without knowledge of the historical contribution of humankind to its construction, its habitat, and its interpretation. One of the major goals of adult education is the reconstruction of personal and collective identity, particularly for marginalised individuals and groups, and adult education must begin with a renewed reading of the environment.

The methodological criteria of a contemporary environmental pedagogy that enables adults to appropriate their identity and to participate in community life. It cannot evade that task for to do so would result in abandoning the role of innovation and transformation that is typical of educational activities, and to be reduced to the status of a tool for the maintenance of the huge contrasts and inequalities that mark the end of this century. The key issues of development are the stuff of adult education, which engages with the social actors involved. Adult education can thus make a crucial contribution in addressing these issues, thereby helping to build, in the creative sense of the term, people's personal and collective identities.

At the European and world level, the issue of the environment—in both its natural and its man-made dimensions—is among the most significant development issues. It is to be henceforward recognised that one of the major threats of the current phase in the development of world society is the progressive degradation of natural and man-made environments. The social, economic, and cultural conflicts that still persist today at national and local levels are beginning to have world-wide repercussions, and they reflect the difficulties experienced by different societies and cultures in living side by side over vast areas of the planet.

The construction of personal and collective identity, and the building of world citizenship, come up against forms of social, economic, and cultural integration that have preserved undiluted the relationships of subservience and dependency that affect the social classes at greatest risk, the weakest cultural communities, and the economically least favoured regions of the South and East. The whole territory of the European continent, like those of the other continents, can be seen as home to many different cultures and societies which, over time, have adapted their diverse natural environments to human ends. They have built their group identity on these environments and have given expression to their supremacy in agreement -though more often in disagreement—with the societies and cultures of the neighbouring territories, and also with those of the same territory. This attachment to local roots, and the patchwork of societies and cultures within one and the same territory, have led to the formation of particularly complex natural, social, and cultural environments.

The modifications to nature and the stratification of human intervention have proved exceptionally severe and far-reaching. In any given territory, they provide characteristic evidence of the way in which humanity and nature have lived together over the years. Such evidence can be seen in the dynamic organisation of life that is characteristic of the human groups that still inhabit a particular territory, whether the macro-region of a national society or the micro-region of a local society, the expression of one or more cultural aggregations.

The people of the new millennium seem more than ever willing to feel once again that they belong to the world that surrounds them. The improvement in global conditions has not gone hand in hand with increased security in community life, either in terms of a consolidation of a feeling of self and of the overall well-being of the individual, or in terms of the cohesion and solidarity of the group or groups. The continual, growing, and often alarming depersonalisation of the individual and the group is affecting a wide range of people and is marginalising them economically, socially, and culturally.

The key issues of development on this continent and around the world therefore demand that a crucial role be given to the building of the personal and collective identity of the population, in particular among the groups that are experiencing the worst disruption to their marginal position in society. Adult education can play an important part by addressing both the natural and the man-made aspects of the issue of the environment as a learning priority, both in formal and in non-formal education.

The key issues of the development of the local and regional community and its environment are the subject matter and the goal of education and training. Through the educational act of discovering and rediscovering the environmental heritage of the territory and its inhabitants, the individual and the local community are engaged in a task of cultural self-knowledge and hence of the enlargement of their own personal and collective identity, and are called on to play an active and original part in the development of the area and in the well-being of the collective itself. To this end, it is important that adult education programmes should take into account not only the most elevated and highly esteemed manifestations of culture in the environment, but also those that are less far-sighted and are usually less well known because they are thought less significant.

It is not unusual for the forces of creative renewal to work through the silences and the least audible and least heard voices in the environment, which, like their marginalised owners, are lost if no light is shed on them and no regard is paid to them. The key issues of local development which a reading of the natural and man-made environment raises and interprets are thus the objective of education and training, in accordance with the theory and practice of 'environmental education.' If approached from this angle, the dilemma of building either a personal or a collective identity can be resolved by finding out, firstly, whether people end up losing their own room for freedom and creativity by adopting the values of the group, with all the dangers of authoritarian denial of will attendant on such a development, or, secondly, whether the collective dimension is having to bend to the requirements of the individual by legitimising the most extreme individualism.

This dichotomy is generally overcome if the individual and the community accept each other in the project of global environmental development, which naturally sheds light on, rather than obscuring, the contradictions and interests of the parties, while showing up directions for solidarity and bringing together the forces of renewal. If adult education does in fact pay attention to the nature, culture, and the developmental problems of the rediscovered territory, it engages individuals, groups of adults, and the entire local community in the task of getting to know and appropriating their own culture and the other cultures present in the territory. This involves overcoming all preconceived discrimination and seizing the opportunity to recognise the most significant human meanings among the cultural evidence that had been overlooked. If individuals, especially those most exposed to marginality and anonymity, enter into communication with these meanings, they more easily find reasons for making contact with and rooting themselves in reality.

Adult education thus makes a specific contribution to adults: it assists them in building and enriching a stronger, more open personal and collective identity based on broadened knowledge and a recognition of— and allegiance to—the natural environment and its varied cultures. Through environmental education, adult education can achieve a further aim that is closely linked to what has gone before. Adults, especially those occupying weaker or more subservient positions in society, are called on to 'reactivate' themselves, to become actors because their reality of life is recognised and because it is they themselves who will, by decoding the signs of the environment and cultural self-knowledge, seek and produce the most original human meanings.

Thus adult education is an integral part of the recent trend to the rediscovery of the environment, which enables individuals to free themselves from immoderate consumption, and which counters the strengthening of discrimination and the mass treatment of people at both the local and the global levels. Environmental education does not merely formulate general principles on the 'A to Z' of the environment, but tries to translate these into educational activities for adults. There were number of methodological criteria that may be used by educators to facilitate the creation of knowledge among adults by using the A to Z of the environment.

The educators — teachers, facilitators, advisers - who use this A to Z of phenomena are concerned both with the evidence of the natural, social, and cultural environment to be found throughout a given territory, and with the public whose attention they call to this evidence. In each case, the education will be conducted differently. In the case of the evidence (whether an archaeological site, items in a museum, a monument, a square or buildings, a river or a marsh), the approach is not enumerative, effect-seeking, and undifferentiated, but constructive, lively, and targeted.

As for the public, educators must be careful to develop a sense of search and discovery, not merely restricting themselves to recording information. That means that the public must not simply take note of the subject matter that is presented to it; the information must not be revealed all at once, but gradually brought out at the instigation of the educator. Such an approach elicits personal attachment and participation, as opposed to an attitude of withdrawal from and indifference towards the heritage sites visited. The educator must elicit and foster attachment and participation - mental and emotional involvement on the part of the public.

Relationships with monuments, archaeological sites, and more generally with the natural and cultural environment must be approached through perception and emotions: visitors are invited to remap space in their minds and to travel in time, so as to understand the people who lived in the age being studied. Particular importance must be accorded to aspects of everyday life, to customs, and to the difficulties encountered by society in a given location and period. The more the visitors encounter problems similar to those that concern them in everyday life, the more they will be able to understand the culture being presented, even if the problems have been resolved differently. The pedagogical and methodological principles set out above need to be translated into operational procedures in order to produce specific educational activities.

The constructivist approach is based on the educational principle according to which the individual builds his or her own education. Through his or her experience of learning, the individual elaborates the knowledge which he or she already has and arrives at new cognitive and non-cognitive syntheses that may be transferred to other contexts of experience. Each learner brings his or her baggage to every stage of teaching, corresponding in this case to different points in the development of the 'journey into the environment.'

Obviously the educator's activities must take this factor into account during the various stages of teaching. The educator must refer to it systematically in order to avoid the danger of losing touch with the knowledge possessed by his or her public. In this way, the educator ensures that the learners feel involved at a cognitive and non-cognitive level and actively participate in the intended journey. This criterion is especially important in the initial stage of teaching. If cognitive and non-cognitive communication with learners is not established from the inception of teaching, they will not be motivated to follow the path. They will also experience difficulties in learning because the information given and the way in which it is presented - particularly the language used - will not resonate with their way of seeing and perceiving things.

It is therefore imperative to refer to learners' knowledge - to their patterns of thought, their fields of perception and emotions, their familiar worlds and language - in order to implement the pedagogy of discovery, participation, and creativity, centred essentially on the learner and his or her process of educational growth. Culture is a subject that is taught in its own right; the teaching is of a slightly different type from that of traditional subjects, but aims in the same way to provide new content.

We have already spoken about environmental evidence as a heritage of knowledge, the meanings of which have to be spelled out - that is, the 'unknown' messages of the unfamiliar. These messages are the new subject matter to be learned. As educational activities unfold, in non-formal education but even more in formal education, the treatment of new knowledge, to which the public must have access, is an indispensable pillar of the edifice, not a secondary factor. Particular attention must therefore be paid to the selection and organisation of the subject matter to be transmitted.

The information to be provided must be evaluated for its meaning in terms of the evidence, but also in terms of the subject matter taught. Some knowledge does not help to define the object; other information reveals its fundamental messages. In the second case, we need to evaluate the information in terms of the perspective we adopt to examine the object. The information may be elementary, but it may also have a structural function in the analytical framework, as in the case of basic concepts of a historical, economic, artistic, or biological nature, or relating to any other teaching subject. These two requirements naturally have to be combined and adapted to the knowledge system of the learner.

Thus the educator is simply extending and enriching that system through the communication which the learner succeeds in establishing with the new information on the environmental evidence of the 'journey.' Learners must not be content with the mere acquisition of new knowledge; they must succeed in internalising new points of view. In other words, learners enter into the reasoning of the discipline that decodes the evidence. They internalise it gradually, progressively, and in proportion to the depth of detail that the educational programme offers; they acquire the basic structural aspects of the analysis, and they reorganise their previous points of view.

Learners thus restructure their cognitive field. The structural aspects of the subject and the structuring effects of the learning combine to cause change in the learner. The process of internalising knowledge contributes to the development of the participation and the creativity fostered by this pedagogy, because it encourages learners to produce new knowledge. The fourth and last reference criterion is that of the transfer of learning. The structuring of new knowledge in the learner through this type of educational journey must be verified, consolidated, and expanded. The process of internalisation of knowledge has its own internal development.

Learners will not succeed in mastering the use of knowledge in an immediate and definitive manner. They will reach that point gradually, and as the process advances, the presence of new knowledge in the learner will improve and take firmer root. If new knowledge is merely juxtaposed with previous knowledge, learners will be unable to use it and will eventually abandon it. It is therefore important for the educator, having provided new knowledge about the environmental evidence, to elicit responses from the learner which show the extent of assimilation and internalisation.

Genuine transfer of learning occurs when learners who have acquired knowledge of a specific subject, situation, or event are able to 'read' and interpret other similar objects, situations, and events. Only then can it be said that the process of internalisation is taking effect. The teacher must allocate well-defined times for 'personal return' by the learner to the evidence being studied, and must also provide opportunities for learners to test themselves. The educator invites the learners to examine other aspects of the evidence (of the building, the monument, or the nature park, for instance) and to formulate a point of view.

Together, teacher and learner discuss the nature of this point of view, and the ability to transfer knowledge is evaluated. Where gaps or uncertainties appear, the educator will be able to take action for subsequent cognitive reinforcement and assessment of learning. The pedagogy of research, participation, and self-expression finds its realisation in the transfer of learning. For each of the criteria mentioned below, it is possible to find a series of technical operations that derive from it and make it possible to move from theory to practice.

A variety of technical solutions can be adopted for assessing learners' knowledge before they begin a programme of environmental education: these may range from a rigidly constructed procedure to a more participatory approach; the former will make it possible to collect quantitative information, and the latter, qualitative information. New knowledge can be supported through various channels that refer both to the content to be conveyed and to the learners who are to appropriate it. The first channel is naturally the phenomenon itself, which might find expression, for example, through a monument or a green space: the visitor's first contact with it through the senses (sight, touch, hearing any sound it makes, and perceiving any smell) provides the initial subjective, personal knowledge of it. But, as is well known, this is not sufficient to decode the evidence.

The transmission of knowledge relating to these phenomena may be made orally or in writing, using words or pictures, depending on whether an explanation of the environmental or cultural phenomenon is given orally by an expert, or particular teaching aids or multimedia tools are used. In order to structure the new knowledge, learners must patiently decode the environmental phenomenon through learning activities allowing them to grasp the 'architecture,' the fundamental aspects, of the phenomenon under study. They must move from a superficial and indistinct knowledge of the environmental or cultural phenomenon to a specific, enriched knowledge through their own interpretation and reflection. They must not be content merely to acquire information that is stored in their 'system' of reading reality.

The mental operations to be carried out will vary according to the problem of interpretation of the environmental phenomenon, the discipline that is used to explore the problem, and the degree of learning reached by the learners. The transfer of learning can in the final analysis be seen in the teaching exercises which enable the learner to use the new knowledge. It is true that in actual teaching practice it is not possible to clearly detach the operations relating to the structuring of new knowledge from those that aim at the transfer of knowledge. The learning of knowledge is not something mechanical, but follows the learner's internal rhythms and dynamics.

6

Teaching of Evolutionary Biology

Humans have always noticed the similarities among closely related species, but it gradually became apparent that even distantly related species share many anatomical and functional characteristics. The bones in a whale's front flippers are arranged in much the same way as the bones in our own arms. As organisms grow from fertilised egg cells into embryos, they pass through many similar developmental stages. Furthermore, as paleontologists studied the fossil record, they discovered countless extinct species that are clearly related in various ways to organisms living today. From bacteria to yeast to mice to humans, all living things use the same biochemical machinery to carry out the basic processes of life.

Many of the proteins that make up cells and catalyse chemical reactions in the body are virtually identical across species. Certain human genes that code for proteins differ little from the corresponding genes in fruit flies, mice, and primates. All living things use the same biochemical system to pass genetic information from one generation to another. From a scientific standpoint, there is one compelling answer to questions about life's commonalities. Different kinds of organisms share so many characteristics of structure and function because they are related to one another.

Investigations of forest ecosystems have helped reveal the incredible diversity of earth's living things.

The concept of biological evolution addresses both of these fundamental questions. It accounts for the relatedness among organisms by explaining that the millions of different species of plants, animals, and microorganisms that live on earth today are related by descent from common ancestors—like distant cousins. Organisms in nature typically produce more offspring than can survive and reproduce given the constraints of food, space, and other resources in the environment. These offspring often differ from one another in ways that are heritable—that is, they can pass on the differences genetically to their own offspring.

If competing offspring have traits that are advantageous in a given environment, they will survive and pass on those traits. As differences continue to accumulate over generations, populations of organisms diverge from their ancestors. This straightforward process, which is a natural consequence of biologically reproducing organisms competing for limited resources, is responsible for one of the most magnificent chronicles known to science. Over billions of years, it has led the earliest organisms on earth to diversify into all of the plants, animals, and microorganisms that exist today. Though humans, fish, and bacteria would seem to be so different as to defy comparison, they all share some of the characteristics of their common ancestors. Evolution also explains the great diversity of modern species.

Populations of organisms with characteristics enabling them to occupy ecological niches not occupied by similar organisms have a greater chance of surviving. Living fish and fossil fish share many similarities, but the fossil fish clearly belongs to a different species that no longer exists. The progression of species found in the fossil record provides powerful evidence for evolution. Evolution explains something else as well. During the billions of years that life has been on earth, it has played an increasingly important role in altering the planet's physical environment. For example, the composition of our atmosphere is partly a consequence of living systems.

During photosynthesis, which is a product of evolution, green plants absorb carbon dioxide and water, produce organic compounds, and release oxygen. This process has created and continues to maintain an atmosphere rich in oxygen. Living communities also profoundly affect weather and the movement of water among the oceans, atmosphere, and land. Much of the rainfall in the forests of the western Amazon basin consists of water that has already made one or more recent trips through a living plant. In addition, plants and soil microorganisms exert important controls over global temperature by absorbing or emitting "greenhouse gases" (such as carbon dioxide and methane) that increase the earth's capacity to retain heat. Living things have altered the earth's oceans, land surfaces, and atmosphere.

For example, photosynthetic organisms are responsible for the oxygen that makes up about a fifth of the earth's atmosphere. The rapid accumulation of atmospheric oxygen about 2 billion years ago led to the evolution of more structured eucaryotic cells, which in turn gave rise to multicellular plants and animals. In short, biological evolution accounts for three of the most fundamental features of the world around us: the similarities among living things, the diversity of life, and many features of the physical world we inhabit. Explanations of these phenomena in terms of evolution draw on results from physics, chemistry, geology, many areas of biology, and other sciences.

Thus, evolution is the central organising principle that biologists use to understand the world. To teach biology without explaining evolution deprives students of a powerful concept that brings great order and coherence to our understanding of life. The teaching of evolution also has great practical value for students. Directly or indirectly, evolutionary biology has made many contributions to society. Evolution explains why many human pathogens have been developing resistance to formerly effective drugs and suggests ways of confronting this increasingly serious problem.

Evolutionary biology has also contributed to many important agricultural advances by explaining the relationships among wild and domesticated plants and animals and their natural enemies. An understanding of evolution has been essential in finding and using natural resources, such as fossil fuels, and it will be indispensable as human societies strive to establish sustainable relationships with the natural environment. Such examples can be multiplied many times. Evolutionary research is one of the most active fields of biology today, and discoveries with important practical applications occur on a regular basis. Those who oppose the teaching of evolution in public schools sometimes ask that teachers present "the evidence against evolution."

However, there is no debate within the scientific community over whether evolution occurred, and there is no evidence that evolution has not occurred. Teaching about evolution has another important function. Because some people see evolution as conflicting with widely held beliefs, the teaching of evolution offers educators a superb opportunity to illuminate the nature of science and to differentiate science from other forms of human endeavor and understanding. Those who oppose the teaching of evolution often say that evolution should be taught as a "theory, not as a fact." This statement confuses the common use of these words with the scientific use.

In science, theories do not turn into facts through the accumulation of evidence. Rather, theories are the end points of science. They are understandings that develop from extensive observation, experimentation, and creative reflection. They incorporate a large body of scientific facts, laws, tested hypotheses, and logical inferences. In this sense, evolution is one of the strongest and most useful scientific theories we have. The concept of evolution has an importance in education that goes beyond its power as a scientific explanation. All of us live in a world where the pace of change is accelerating.

Today's children will face more new experiences and different conditions than their parents or teachers have had to face in their lives. The central feature of scientific revolution has been the abandonment of one notion about stability after another: that the earth was the centre of the universe, that the world's living things are unchangeable, that the continents of the earth are held rigidly in place, and so on. Fluidity and change have become central to our understanding of the world around us. To accept the probability of change—and to see change as an agent of opportunity rather than as a threat—is a silent message and challenge in the lesson of evolution.

Issues in Teaching

Teaching evolution presents special challenges to science

teachers. Sources of support upon which teachers can draw include high-quality curricula, adequate preparation, exposure to information useful in documenting the evidence for evolution, and resources and contacts provided by professional associations. One important source of support for teachers is to share problems and explore solutions with other teachers. The world around us changes. This simple fact is obvious everywhere we look. Streams wash dirt and stones from higher places to lower places.

Untended gardens fill with weeds. Other changes are more gradual but much more dramatic when viewed over long time scales. Powerful telescopes reveal new stars coalescing from galactic dust, just as our sun did more than 4.5 billion years ago. The earth itself formed shortly thereafter, when rock, dust, and gas circling the sun condensed into the planets of our solar system. Fossils of primitive microorganisms show that life had emerged on earth by about 3.8 billion years ago. Similarly, the fossil record reveals profound changes in the kinds of living things that have inhabited our planet over its long history.

Trilobites that populated the seas hundreds of millions of years ago no longer crawl about. Mammals now live in a world that was once dominated by reptilian giants such as Tyrannosaurus rex. More than 99 percent of the species that have ever lived on the earth are now extinct, either because all of the members of the species died, the species evolved into a new species, or it split into two or more new species. The Hubble Space Telescope has revealed many astronomical phenomena that ground-based telescopes cannot see.

The images at right show disks of matter around young stars that could give rise to planets. In the image below, stars are forming in the tendrils of gas and dust extending from a gigantic nebula. Many kinds of cumulative change through time have been described by the term "evolution," and the term is used in astronomy, geology, biology, anthropology, and other sciences. The ancient Greeks were already speculating about the origins of life and changes in species over time. More than 2,500 years ago, the Greek philosopher Anaximander thought that a gradual evolution had created the world's organic coherence from a formless condition, and he had a fairly modern view of the transformation of aquatic species into terrestrial ones.

Charles Darwin, Alfred Russel Wallace, and Gregor Mendel laid the foundations of modern evolutionary theory. During the early 1800s, many naturalists speculated about changes in organisms, especially as geological investigations revealed the rich story laid out in the fossilised remains of extinct creatures. But although ideas about evolution were proposed, they never gained wide acceptance because no one was able to propose a plausible mechanism for how the form of an organism might change from one generation to another. Then, in 1858, two English naturalists—Charles Darwin and Alfred Russel Wallace—simultaneously issued papers proposing such a mechanism.

Both men observed that the individual members of a particular species are not identical but can differ in many ways. For example, some will be able to run a little faster, have a different colour, or respond to the same circumstance in different ways. Both men further observed that many of these differences are inherited and can be passed on to offspring. Darwin and Wallace were both deeply influenced by the realisation that, even though most species produce an abundance of offspring, the size of the overall population usually remains about the same. Thus, an oak tree might produce many thousands of acorns each year, but few, if any, will survive to become full-grown trees.

Darwin—who conceived of his ideas in the 1830s but did not publish them until Wallace came to similar conclusions—presented the case for evolution in detail in his 1859 book On the Origin of Species by Natural Selection. Darwin proposed that there will be differences between offspring that survive and reproduce and those that do not. In particular, individuals that have heritable characteristics making them more likely to survive and reproduce in their particular environment will, on average, have a better chance of passing those characteristics on to their own offspring. In this way, as many generations pass, nature would select those individuals best suited to particular environments, a process Darwin called natural selection.

Over very long times, Darwin argued, natural selection acting on varying individuals within a population of organisms could account for all of the great variety of organisms we see today, as well as for the species found as fossils. Darwin did not know that a contemporary, Gregor Mendel, had provided an important part of the solution. In his classic 1865 paper describing crossbreeding of varieties of peas, Mendel demonstrated that organisms acquire traits through discrete units of heredity which later came to be known as genes. The variation produced through these inherited traits is the raw material on which natural selection acts.

Mendel's paper was all but forgotten until 1890, when it was rediscovered and contributed to a growing wave of interest and research in genetics. But it was not immediately clear how to reconcile new findings about the mechanisms of inheritance with evolution through natural selection. Then, in the 1930s, a group of biologists demonstrated how the results of genetics research could both buttress and extend evolutionary theory. They showed that all variations, both slight and dramatic, arose through changes, or mutations, in genes.

If a mutation enabled an organism to survive or reproduce more effectively, that mutation would tend to be preserved and spread in a population through natural selection. Evolution was thus seen to depend both on genetic mutations and on natural selection. Mutations provided abundant genetic variation, and natural selection sorted out the useful changes from the deleterious ones. Selection by natural processes of favoured variants explained many observations on the geography of species differences—why, for example, members of the same bird species might be larger and darker in the northern part of their range, and smaller and paler in the southern part.

In this case, differences might be explained by the advantages of large size and dark coloration in forested, cold regions. And, if the species occupied the entire range continuously, genes favouring light colour and small size would be able to flow into the northern population, and vice versa—prohibiting their separation into distinct species that are reproductively isolated from one another. In the 1950s, the study of evolution entered a new phase. Biologists began to be able to determine the exact molecular structure of the proteins in living things—that is, the actual sequences of the amino acids that make up each protein. Almost immediately, it became clear that certain proteins that serve the same function in different species have very similar amino acid sequences.

The protein evidence was completely consistent with the idea of a common evolutionary history for the planet's living things. Even more important, this knowledge provided important clues about the history of evolution that could not be obtained through the fossil record. The discovery of the structure of DNA by Francis Crick and James Watson in 1953 extended the study of evolution to the most fundamental level. The sequence of the chemical bases in DNA both specifies the order of amino acids in proteins and determines which proteins are synthesised in which cells. In this way, DNA is the ultimate source of both change and continuity in evolution. The modification of DNA through occasional changes or rearrangements in the base sequences underlies the emergence of new traits, and thus of new species, in evolution.

At the same time, all organisms use the same molecular codes to translate DNA base sequences into protein amino acid sequences. This uniformity in the genetic code is powerful evidence for the interrelatedness of living things, suggesting that all organisms presently alive share a common ancestor that can be traced back to the origins of life on earth. One common misconception among students is that individual organisms change their characteristics in response to the environment. In other words, students often think that the environment acts on individual organisms to generate physical characteristics that can then be passed on genetically to offspring. But selection can work only on the genetic variation that already is present in any new generation, and genetic variation occurs randomly, not in response to the needs of a population or organism. In this sense, as Francois Jacob has written, evolution is a "tinkerer, not an engineer."

Evolution does not design new organisms; rather, new organisms emerge from the inherent genetic variation that occurs in organisms. Genetic variation is random, but natural selection is not. Natural selection tests the combinations of genes represented in the members of a species and allows to proliferate those that confer the greatest ability to survive and reproduce. In this sense, evolution is not the simple product of random chance. Fossils found in rocks of increasing age attest to the interrelated lineage of living things, from the single-celled organisms that lived billions of years ago to Homo sapiens.

The most recent fossils closely resemble the organisms alive today, whereas increasingly older fossils are progressively different, providing compelling evidence of change through time. Even a casual look at different kinds of organisms reveals striking similarities among species, and anatomists have discovered that these similarities are more than skin deep. All vertebrates, for example, from fish to humans, have a common body plan characterised by a segmented body and a hollow main nerve cord along the back.

The best available scientific explanation for these common structures is that all vertebrates are descended from a common ancestor species and that they have diverged through evolution. In the past, evolutionary relationships could be studied only by examining the consequences of genetic information, such as the anatomy, physiology, and embryology of living organisms. But the advent of molecular biology has made it possible to read the history of evolution that is written in every organism's DNA. This information has allowed organisms to be placed into a common evolutionary family tree in a much more detailed way than possible from previous evidence.

The concept of evolution through random genetic variation and natural selection makes sense of what would otherwise be a huge body of unconnected observations. It is no longer possible to sustain scientifically the view that the living things we see today did not evolve from earlier forms or that the human species was not produced by the same evolutionary mechanisms that apply to the rest of the living world. Evolution by natural selection is not only a historical process—it still operates today. For example, the continual evolution of human pathogens has come to pose one of the most serious public health problems now facing human societies.

Many strains of bacteria have become increasingly resistant to once-effective antibiotics as natural selection has amplified resistant strains that arose through naturally occurring genetic variation. The microorganisms that cause malaria, gonorrhea, tuberculosis, and many other diseases have demonstrated greatly increased resistance to the antibiotics and other drugs used to treat them in the past. The continued use and overuse of antibiotics has had the effect of selecting for resistant populations because the antibiotics give these strains an advantage over nonresistant strains. Similar episodes of rapid evolution are occurring in many different organisms. Rats have developed resistance to the poison warfarin.

Many hundreds of insect species and other agricultural pests have evolved resistance to the pesticides used to combat them—and even to chemical defences genetically engineered into plants. Species of plants have evolved tolerance to toxic metals and have reduced their interbreeding with nearby nontolerant plants—an initial step in the formation of separate species. New species of plants have arisen through the crossbreeding of native plants with plants introduced from elsewhere in the world. The North American species Chrysoperla carnea and Chrysoperla downesi separated from a common ancestor species recently in evolutionary time and are very similar. But they are different in colour, reflecting their different habitats, and they breed at different times of the year. The creation of a new species from a pre-existing species generally requires thousands of years, so over a lifetime a single human usually can witness only a tiny part of the speciation process.

Yet even that glimpse of evolution at work powerfully confirms our ideas about the history and mechanisms of evolution. For example, many closely related species have been identified that split from a common ancestor very recently in evolutionary terms. An example is provided by the North American lacewings Chrysoperla carnea and Chrysoperla downesi. The former lives in deciduous woodlands and is pale green in summer and brown in winter. The latter lives among evergreen conifers and is dark green all year round.

The two species are genetically and morphologically very similar. Yet they occupy different habitats and breed at different times of the year and so are reproductively isolated from each other. The fossil record also sheds light on speciation. A particularly dramatic example comes from recently discovered fossil evidence documenting the evolution of whales and dolphins. The fossil record shows that these cetaceans evolved from a primitive group of hoofed mammals called Mesonychids. Some of these mammals crushed and ate turtles, as evidenced by the shape of their teeth. This mammal gave rise to a species with front forelimbs and powerful hind legs with large feet that were adapted for paddling. This animal, known as Ambulocetus, could have moved between sea and land. Its fossilised vertebrae also show that this animal could move its back in a strong up and down motion, which is the method modern cetaceans use to swim and dive.

A later fossil in the series from Pakistan shows an animal with smaller functional hind limbs and even greater back flexibility. This species, Rodhocetus, probably did not venture onto land very often, if at all. Finally, Basilosaurus fossils from Egypt and the United States present a recognisable whale, with front flippers for steering and a completely flexible backbone. But this animal still has hind limbs (thought to have been nonfunctional), which have become further reduced in modern whales. Modern whales evolved from a primitive group of hoofed mammals into species that were progressively more adapted to life in the water. Another focus of research has been the evolution of ancient apelike creatures through many intermediate forms into modern humans.

Homo sapiens, one of 185 known living species in the primate order, is a member of the hominoids, a category that includes orangutans, gorillas, and chimpanzees. The succession of species that would give rise to humans seems to have separated from the succession that would lead to the apes about 5 to 8 million years ago. The first members of our genus, Homo, had evolved by about 1.5 million years ago. According to recent evidence—based on the sequencing of DNA found in a part of human cells known as mitochondria—it has been proposed that a small group of modern humans evolved in Africa about 150,000 years ago and spread throughout the world, replacing archaic populations of Homo sapiens. Early hominids had smaller brains and larger faces than species belonging to the genus Homo, including our own species, Homo sapiens. White parts of the skulls are reconstructions, and the skulls are not all on the same scale.

Animals and plants do not live in isolation, nor do they evolve in isolation. Indeed, much of the pressure toward diversification comes not only from physical factors in the environment but from the presence of other species. Any animal is a potential host for parasites or prey for a carnivore. A plant has other plants as competitors for space and light, can be a host for parasites, and provides food for herbivores. The interactions within the complex communities, or ecosystems, in which organisms live can generate powerful evolutionary forces. Evolution in natural communities arises from both constraints and opportunities.

The constraints come from competitors, primarily among the same species. There are only so many nest holes for bluebirds and so much food for mice. Genetically different individuals that are able to move to a different resource—a new food supply, for example, or a hitherto uninhabited area—are able to exploit that resource free of competition. As a result, the trait that opened up the new opportunity will be favoured by natural selection because the individuals possessing it are able to survive and reproduce better than other members of their species in the new environment. An ecologist would say that the variant had occupied a new niche—a term that defines the "job description" of an organism. (For example, a bluebird would have the niche of insect- and fruit-eater, inhabitant of forest edges and meadows, tree-hole nester, and so on.)

One often finds closely related species in the same place and occupying what look like identical niches. However, if the niches were truly identical, one of the species should have a competitive advantage over the other and eventually drive the less fit species to extinction or to a different niche. That leads to a tentative hypothesis: where we find such a situation, careful observation should reveal subtle niche specialisation of the apparently competing species. This hypothesis has been tested by many biologists. For example, in the 1960s Robert MacArthur carefully studied three North American warblers of the same genus that were regularly seen feeding on insects in coniferous trees in the same areas—indeed, often in the same trees.

MacArthur's painstaking observations revealed that the three were actually specialists: one fed on insects on the major branches near the trunk; another occupied the mid-regions of branches and ate from different parts of the foliage; and the third fed on insects occupying the finest needles near the periphery of the tree. Although the three warblers occurred together, they were in fact not competitors for the same food resources. Often, species that are evolving together in the same ecosystem do so through a highly interactive process. For example, natural selection will favour organisms with defences against predation; in turn, predators experience selection for traits that overcome those defences. Such coevolutionary competitions are common in nature.

Many plants manufacture and store chemicals that deter herbivorous insects; but usually one or more insect species will have evolved biochemical mechanisms for inactivating the deterrent, providing them with a plant they can eat relatively free of competitors. Another classic example of coevolution involves the introduction of rabbits and the myxomatosis virus into Australia. After rabbits were brought to Australia, they multiplied rapidly and threatened the wool industry because they grazed on the same plants as sheep. To control the rabbit population, a virulent pathogen of rabbits, the myxomatosis virus, also was introduced into Australia. Within a decade, rabbits had become more resistant to the virus, and the virus had evolved into a less virulent form, allowing both the host and pathogen to coexist.

Science Teaching

Science is a particular way of knowing about the world. In science, explanations are restricted to those that can be inferred from confirmable data—the results obtained through observations and experiments that can be substantiated by other scientists. Anything that can be observed or measured is amenable to scientific investigation. Explanations that cannot be based on empirical evidence are not a part of science. The history of life on earth is a fascinating subject that can be studied through observations made today, and these observations have led to compelling accounts of how organisms have changed over time.

The best available evidence suggests that life on earth began more than three and a half billion years ago. For more than two billion years after that, life was housed in the bodies of many kinds of tiny, single-celled organisms, some of which produced the oxygen that now makes up more than a fifth of the earth's atmosphere. Less than a billion years ago, much more complex organisms appeared.

By about half a billion years ago, evolution had resulted in a wide variety of multicellular animals and plants living in the sea that are the clear ancestors of many of the major types of organisms that continue to live to this day. Somewhat more than 400 million years ago, some marine plants and animals began one of the greatest of all innovations in evolution—they invaded dry land. For our own phylum, the Chordata, this move away from the nurturing sea led to the appearance of amphibians, reptiles, birds, and mammals—the latter including, of course, our own species, Homo sapiens.

Surely one of the first major natural phenomena to be understood was the cause of night and day. Some of the earliest surviving human records left on clay tablets relate to the movements of the sun and other celestial bodies. The obvious cause of day and night is the rising and setting of the sun. This is an observation that can be made today by anyone and, seemingly, requires no further explanation. Archaeological evidence and early records make it clear that our ancestors realised that not only does the sun appear to rise and set, but so do the moon and stars.

The movements of the moon and stars, however, are not precisely synchronised with those of the sun. The moon is slower by about one hour per day. The stars remain almost the same on successive nights, but slowly it becomes obvious that they, too, are slowed in their movements compared to the sun. Thus, the stars of summer are different from those visible in the winter. In fact, it takes a full year for the stars to return to their previous position, an interval of time that defines our year. The ancient observers realised that not all stars move in unison. Although most move in majestic unity, a few others are "wanderers"—appearing now with one group of stars and a week later somewhere else. The majority were called "fixed stars," the wanderers were called "planets."

Nicolaus Copernicus, Johannes Kepler, Galileo Galilei, and Isaac Newton led the way to a new understanding of the relationship between the earth and the sun and initiated an age of scientific progress that continues today. During the late Middle Ages, and especially in the Renaissance, beautiful brass models known as orreries were made to show the relative positions and movements of the sun, planets, and moon as they circled the earth. As the centre of the universe, the earth was a sphere in the centre of the orrery. The other celestial bodies were positioned on rings of metal, each moving by clockwork at its own rate. The fixed stars required a simple solution—they could be considered stuck in an outermost shell, also moved by clockwork. The problem with orreries—and with the theories of the cosmos then prevailing—was that they had to become successively more complex as more became known.

Careful observations of the movements of the stars and planets greatly complicated the hypotheses used to account for those movements. This growing complexity stimulated some of the leading astronomers of the 16th and 17th centuries, including Copernicus, Kepler, and Galileo, to make even more precise observations of the movements of the heavenly bodies. Astronomers used these measurements to demonstrate that the age-old human explanations of the heavens were incomplete. In the process, they replaced a complex and confusing explanation with a simple one: the sun, rather than the earth, is at the centre of a "solar system," and the earth revolves around it. That simple step—a bold departure from past thinking due mainly to the insights of Copernicus —dramatically changed the picture of the then known universe. This concept of heliocentricism initially ran counter to the positions of religious authorities.

The view of Christianity over most of its history, based on a literal interpretation of the Bible, was that the earth is the centre of the universe around which the celestial bodies revolve. Copernicus dedicated his book describing the theory of heliocentricism, De revolutionibus orbium coelestium, to Pope Paul III and promptly died. That saved him the troubles that were to beset Galileo (1564 to 1642), whose astronomical observations confirmed the views of Copernicus. Galileo was told to abandon his beliefs, and he later was tried by the Inquisition and sentenced to the equivalent of house arrest.

The Church held that his views were dangerous to faith. Continued study and ever more careful measurements of the movements of the planets and sun continued to support the heliocentric hypothesis. Then, in the latter half of the 17th century, Isaac Newton (1642 to 1727) showed that the force of gravity—as measured on the earth—could account for the movements of the planets given the laws of motion that Newton derived. As a result of the steady accumulation of evidence, the theological interpretation of celestial movements gave way to the naturalistic explanation, and it is now accepted that night and day are the consequences of the rotation of the earth on its axis.

Today, we can see for ourselves the rotation of the earth from satellites orbiting the planet. Illustration from the 18th century depicts the Ptolemaic system in the upper left corner and the Copernican system in other corners and centre. Like biological evolution, the theory of heliocentricism brought order and new understanding to an otherwise chaotic and confusing aspect of nature. It also had great practical applications, in that the exploration of the world by European seafarers used the more accurate understanding of celestial mechanics to assist in navigation.

Looking at the night sky remains a powerful experience. But that experience is now informed not only by the beauty and majesty of the heavens, but by a deeper understanding of nature and by an appreciation of the power of the human intellect. The human mind says a great deal about the nature of science.

First, science is not the same as common sense. Common sense indicates that the sun does rise and set. Nevertheless, there can be other explanations of that phenomenon, and one of them, the rotation of the earth on its axis, is responsible for day and night. A concept based on observation proved to need extensive modification as new observations accumulated.

Second, the statements of science should never be accepted as "final truth." Instead, over time they generally form a sequence of increasingly more accurate statements. Nevertheless, in the case of heliocentricism as in evolution, the data are so convincing that the accuracy of the theory is no longer questioned in science.

Third, scientific progress depends on individuals, but the contributions of one individual could be made by others. If Copernicus had kept his ideas to himself, the discovery of heliocentricism would have been postponed, but it would not have been blocked, since other astronomers eventually would have come to the same conclusion. Similarly, had Darwin and Wallace not published their hypotheses, the concept of biological evolution would nevertheless have emerged as the accepted explanation for the history of life on earth. The same cannot be said in other areas of human endeavor; for example, had Shakespeare never published, we would most assuredly never have had his plays.

The publications of scientists, unlike those of playwrights, are a means to an end—they are not the end itself. What are the scientific methods that have led to our current understanding of the history of life over vast eons of time? They begin with careful descriptions of the material being studied. The material for the study of biological evolution is life itself. One basic aspect of life is that individuals can be grouped as similar kinds, or species. Another important observation is that many species seem to be closely related to each other.

The scientific classification of species and their arrangement into groups began with the publication in 1758 of Systema Naturae, or system of nature, by the Swedish naturalist Carolus Linnaeus (1707 to 1778). For example, Linnaeus knew seven dog-like species, and he gave each a double name. Subsequently many more species were discovered and some of the names were changed—and continue to be changed as more information is obtained. The domestic dog is Canis familiaris; the coyote of North America is Canis latrans; the Australian dingo is Canis dingo; and the wolf of the northern hemisphere is Canis lupus. Thus Canis is the name of the genus of dog-like animals, and the distinctive second name is the species name.

Generations of scientists have discovered new species, described them, and arranged them into the system first suggested by Linnaeus. Whereas Linnaeus recognised about 9,000 species, systematists now have recognised about 1.5 million. The task of categorising and describing species is still far from complete. Most species of smaller invertebrates, and many bacteria and other microscopic organisms, remain to be discovered. The plant kingdom is also incompletely known. Though the flowering plants of many areas, such as Europe and North America, are fairly well described, many other regions have not been nearly as well explored by botanists.

Recent investigations in the exceptionally diverse rainforests of South America have caused biologists to raise their estimates of the number of undescribed species. For example, a very high proportion of insects collected from the forest canopy are "new" species to science. It is now believed that the number of different species of plants and animals in the world may be ten million, or even more. The scientific methods used in classifying organisms have been greatly improved over time. The process begins with the intensive field work in which the animals, plants, and microorganisms are collected and carefully examined.

Most will be known to a specialist, but there might be some unusual examples. However, none is likely to be a complete stranger, since the specialist will probably recognise that any puzzling specimen is similar to some familiar species. Next the specialist must check all that has been published on the group of organisms that contains the similar species. If, after an exhaustive search, there is no record of a described species that corresponds to the one being examined, the specimen is probably a new species. The specialist will then prepare a careful description of the new species and publish it in a scientific journal.

There is a permanent reward for being the describer of a new species: thereafter monographs that deal with the classification of the group to which the new species belongs will add the describer's name at the end of the scientific name. Thus, for example, "Homo sapiens Linnaeus" is our own proper identification, because Linnaeus was the first to give us our scientific name. This example makes it clear that not all scientific data are derived as the result of experimentation. The conventional classification of species into seemingly natural groups involved the careful observation of a variety of different species, followed by the use of selected characteristics in an attempt to define groups of species thought to be related.

But the groupings are not always obvious. For example, it might have seemed reasonable to classify bats with birds, since the most conspicuous characteristic of each is the ability to fly. But bats are mammals. Like all mammals, their bodies are covered with hair and their young are born alive (instead of hatching from eggs) and are nourished by milk from the mother's mammary glands. Although most of the species we know today were described after the time of Linnaeus, we continue to use his basic system of hierarchical classification. For example, similar genera are united in families, similar families in orders, similar orders in classes, and similar classes in phyla.

The dog-like species listed above (the genus Canis), plus a number of similar but more distant dog-like animals, are grouped as the family Canidae. This family plus the families of cats, bears, seals, and weasels form the order Carnivora. The carnivores and all other animals with hair are combined as the class Mammalia. Mammals are combined with the birds, reptiles, amphibians, fishes, plus some small marine animals in the phylum Chordata. Today, many systematists group organisms according to a system known as cladistics. By determining which traits of a species evolved earlier and which evolved later, this system seeks to classify organisms according to their evolutionary history.

In the quest for understanding, science involves a great deal of careful observation that eventually produces an elaborate written description of the natural world. This description is communicated to scientists in scientific journals or at scientific meetings, so that others can build on pre-existing work. In this way, the accuracy and sophistication of the description tends to increase with time, as subsequent generations of scientists correct and extend the observations of their predecessors. Because the total sum of scientific knowledge increases relentlessly, scientific progress is something that all scientists take for granted. But science is not just description. Even as observations are being made, the human mind attempts to sort, or organise, the observations in a way that reveals some underlying order in the objects or phenomena being observed. This sorting process, which involves a great deal of trial and error, seems to be driven by a fundamental human urge to make sense of our world.

The sorting process also suggests new observations that might otherwise not be made. For example, the suggestion that bats should be grouped with mammals led to an intensified examination of the similarities between bats and rodents—first at the anatomical level, and later with respect to the genes and protein molecules that form their cells. In this case, new evidence was obtained that confirmed the suggested relationship. In other cases, the further observations inspired by a tentative grouping have caused the rejection of a new idea. The realisation that species can be arranged in a hierarchy of groups of seemingly similar forms raised an obvious question: What accounts for the relatedness of different groups of organisms?

The mechanism that was proposed by Darwin directly addressed this question. It suggested that all animals classified as belonging to the same group had a common ancestor species. That is, dogs, wolves, coyotes and all members of the genus Canis are descended from a common ancestor species that lived in the remote past. In a similar manner all species in a family, an order, a class, or a phylum share a common inheritance. In the decades before Darwin proposed his hypothesis, geologists realised that the sedimentary rocks of the earth's crust contain a running diary of earth's history. This record of past events comes about because the earth's crust is in a constant state of change. This observation might not be obvious in the lifetime of an individual, but it is dramatic over thousands of years.

Relatively flat surfaces are uplifted to form mountains, and then the mountains slowly erode to form flatlands. Storms produce powerful waves that erode cliffs at the seashore. These phenomena have the common feature of moving solid materials, and the subsequent settling out of these materials makes possible the formation of a special form of rock that contains a record of the earth's past. Consider the case of a river with a source in the mountains. As the water moves downstream, it erodes the slopes of the mountains. Tiny grains produced by the erosion, called silt, are relatively easy to move.

When the river reaches the flatlands, a lake, or the ocean, the solid material being carried by the water is deposited—often reaching great thicknesses over long periods of time. Then the pressure of the sediments on top can cause the sediments beneath to harden into "sedimentary rocks." The river may carry things other than silt, sand, and rocks. Hard structures of organisms such as the bones and teeth of animals may be carried along as well. These, too, will be deposited with the silt, sand, and rocks. Under certain circumstances, these remains of organisms undergo a chemical change in which the original material is replaced by molecules that form stone. In this way, the organic remains of living things are fossilised (changed into stone), creating the evidence of ancient life studied by scientists.

Because of the order in which the sediments are deposited, the most recent layer of rocks normally will be on top and the oldest layer will be on the bottom (though sometimes sediments are flipped upside down by the geologic folding of rock layers). Also, the fossils in each layer usually will be of those organisms that lived at the time the layer was formed. Thus, the fossils in the lower layers will represent species that lived earlier than those found in the upper layers. The relative position of fossils tells only which are older and which younger. One can estimate the difference in the ages of the two fossils by noting the thickness of the rock that separates them.

If the difference is only one foot, one might guess the interval of time is less than if two fossils are separated by 50 feet of rock layers. Today, however, far more accurate methods of dating fossils are available, as described on the next page. Because these methods are based on the known rates of radioactive decay, they provide valuable measures of absolute time. The scientific study of fossils is called paleontology, and the methods used for their identification and classification are similar to those used for living species. But in some respects the task of the paleontologist is far more difficult. Many species lack hard parts such as bones and shells, and such organisms almost always decay without becoming fossilised. This is the case for many groups of soft-bodied invertebrates—such as worms of many kinds, jellyfish, and protozoans.

Even for such species as mammals, birds, reptiles, and amphibians, death is usually followed by the skeleton being dismembered and the bones scattered. For this reason, whereas isolated bones are often fossilised, it is exceptionally rare for an intact skeleton to be found. Tiny fossils first reveal the existence of bacteria 3.5 to 3.8 billion years ago, and animals composed of more than a single cell are known from about 670 million years ago. But the organisms that lived between these two dates lacked hard parts and, hence, were rarely preserved as fossils. Then, about 570 million years ago, a dramatic change took place. At the beginning of the Cambrian period, animals evolved that had calcified shells and other types of body coverings that had a far better chance of becoming fossilised. These fossils demonstrate that Cambrian seas were populated with a variety of invertebrates.

The earliest vertebrate fossils date from about 500 million years ago. Thereafter early amphibians and reptiles appeared. Birds and mammals appear in the fossil record only about 200 million years ago, while dinosaurs first appear about 225 million years ago and disappear suddenly about 160 million years later. In the fossil record, most species are characterised by a specific appearance, a duration over time, and extinction. The evolutionary origins of species are inferred from the morphological relations among fossils. In the 1830s, when Darwin began his studies, the essential features of the fossil record were known (although absolute dates had not yet been determined).

Many thousands of living species had been described, and it was clearly recognised that they could be organised into various groups—suggesting that they are somehow relatives. In addition, analysis of the fossil record revealed that the organisms on the ancient earth had undergone major changes over time—with whole groups of animals appearing, persisting for long periods of time, and then disappearing. Darwin was an unusually keen observer. But he was not content to catalogue facts and observations. Instead, the natural world to him was a gigantic, very challenging puzzle that demanded an explanation for its otherwise bewildering complexity. Certain observations seemed particularly important.

For example: In South America, the only continent where living armadillos were found, Darwin discovered fossil evidence for the prior existence of ancient species that had many of the unique features of living armadillos, yet were clearly different. Such fossils were found nowhere else in the world. Why were both living and ancient armadillo-like species confined to the same geographical region? One of the greatest scientific triumphs of the last two centuries has been the discovery of the vast expanse of geologic time.

Early methods of calculating the age of the earth relied on measures of the rate of sedimentation or the cooling of the earth from an initially molten state. The relative ages of rocks also were calculated early in the 1800s by noting what kinds of fossils the rocks contained. But the absolute age of the earth and the timing of many events in geologic history required the discovery late in the 19th century of a previously unknown phenomenon: radioactivity. Some elements, such as uranium, undergo radioactive decay to produce other elements. By measuring the quantities of radioactive elements and the elements into which they decay in rocks, geologists can determine how much time has elapsed since the rock cooled from an initially molten state.

For example, the oldest known rocks are found in Greenland and date from about 3.8 billion years ago. Scientists believe the earth's age to be about 4.6 billion years because meteorites and rocks of the moon—both of which formed about the same time as the earth—date from this time. Radiometric dating also shows that the period of earth's history during which large fossils can be readily found in rocks began only about 570 million years ago. Radiometric dating draws on information and insights from many areas of science. For example, it requires that the rate of radioactive decay is constant over time and is not influenced by such factors as temperature or pressure—conclusions supported by extensive research in physics.

It also assumes that the rocks being analysed have not been altered over time by the migration of atoms into or out of the rocks, which requires detailed information from both the geologic and chemical sciences. On the Galapagos Islands, 600 miles off the coast of Ecuador, Darwin observed many distinct living species of birds and reptiles that closely resembled each other—yet were different on each tiny island. Why, for example, should the beak size of the mockingbirds on one island be different from that of a closely related mockingbird on an island only 30 miles away?

And why were the various types of animals on these islands related, but distinct from, the animals in Ecuador, whereas those on the otherwise very similar islands off the coast of Africa were related to the animals in Africa instead? Darwin could not see how these observations could be explained by the prevailing view of his time: that each species had been independently created, with the species that were best suited to each location on the earth being created at each particular site. It looked instead as though species could evolve from one into another over time, with each being confined to the particular geographical region where its ancestors happened to be—particularly if isolated by major barriers to migration, such as vast expanses of ocean. But how could one species turn into another over the course of time? In constructing his hypothesis of how this occurred, Darwin was struck by several other observations that he and others before him had made.

People who bred domesticated animals and plants for commercial or recreational use had found and exploited a great deal of variation among the progeny of their crosses. Pigeon breeders, for example, had observed wide differences in colors, beaks, necks, feet, and tails of the offspring from a single mating pair. They routinely enhanced their stocks for desired traits—for example, selectively breeding those animals that shared a particular type of beak. Through such artificial selection, pigeon fanciers had been able to create many different-looking pigeons, known as breeds. A similar type of artificial selection for mating pairs of dogs had likewise created the whole variety of shapes and sizes of these common pets—ranging from a Great Dane to a dachshund. Animals living in the wild can face a tremendous struggle for survival.

For some birds, for example, fewer than one in 100 animals born in one year will survive over a harsh winter into a second year. Those with characteristics best suited for a particular environment—for example, those individual birds who are best able to find scarce food in the winter while avoiding becoming food for a larger animal – tend to have better chances of surviving. Darwin called this process natural selection to distinguish it from the artificial selection used by dog and pigeon breeders to determine which animals to mate to produce offspring.

At least 20 years elapsed between the time that Darwin conceived of descent with modification and 1859, the year that he revealed his ideas to the world in On the Origin of Species. Throughout these 20 years, Darwin did what scientists today do: he tested his ideas of how things work with new observations and experiments. In part, he did this by thinking up every possible objection he could to his own hypothesis. For each such argument, Darwin tried to find an observation made by others, make an observation, or do an experiment of his own that might imply that his ideas were in fact not valid. When he could successfully counter such objections, he strengthened his theory.

For example, Darwin's ideas readily explained why distant oceanic islands were generally devoid of terrestrial mammals, except for flying bats. But how could the land snails, so common on such islands, have traversed the hundreds of miles of open ocean that separate the islands from the mainland where the snails first evolved? By floating snails on salt-water for prolonged periods, Darwin convinced himself that, on rare occasions in the past, snails might in fact have "floated in chunks of drifted timber across moderately wide arms of the sea." This example shows how a hypothesis can drive a scientist to do experiments that would otherwise not be done.

Prior to Darwin, the existence of land snails and bats, but not typical terrestrial mammals, on the oceanic islands was simply noted and catalogued as a fact. It is unlikely that anyone would have thought to test the snails for their ability to survive for prolonged periods in salt water. Even if they had, such an experiment would have had little meaning or impact. By publishing his ideas, Darwin subjected his hypothesis to the tests of others. This process of public scrutiny is an essential part of science. It works to eliminate individual bias and subjectivity, because others must also be able to determine whether a proposed explanation is consistent with the available evidence.

It also leads to further observations or to experiments designed to test hypotheses, which has the effect of advancing science. Many of the hypotheses advanced by scientists turn out to be incorrect when tested by further observations or experiments. But skillful scientists like Darwin tend to have good ideas that end up increasing the amount of knowledge in the world. For this reason, the ideas of scientists have been—over the long run—central to much of human progress. At the time of Darwin, there were many unsolved puzzles, including missing links in the fossil record between major groups of animals.

Guided by the central idea of evolution, thousands of scientists have spent their lives searching for evidence that either supports or conflicts with the idea. For example, since Darwin's time, paleontologists have discovered many ancient organisms that connect major groups—such as Archaeopteryx between ancient reptiles and birds, and Ichthyostega between ancient fish and amphibians. By now, so much evidence has been found that supports the fundamental idea of biological evolution that its occurrence is no longer questioned in science.

Even more striking has been the information obtained during the 20th century from studies on the molecular basis of life. The theory of evolution implies that each organism should contain detailed molecular evidence of its relative place in the hierarchy of living things. This evidence can be found in the DNA sequences of living organisms. Before a cell can divide to produce two daughter cells, it must make a new copy of its DNA.

Theory of Plate Tectonics

The theory of plate tectonics demonstrates that revolutions in science are not just a thing of the past, thus suggesting that more revolutions can be expected in the future. World maps have long indicated a curious "jigsaw puzzle fit" of the continents. This is especially apparent between the facing coastlines of South America and Africa. Alfred Wegener, a German meteorologist who was dissatisfied with explanations that relied on expanding and contracting crust to account for mountain building and the formation of the ocean floor, pursued other lines of reasoning. Wegener suggested that all of earth's continents used to be assembled in a single ancient super-continent he called Pangea. He hypothesised that Pangea began to break up approximately 200 million years ago, with South America and Africa slowly drifting apart to their present positions, leaving the southern Atlantic Ocean between them. This was an astonishing hypothesis: could huge continents really move?

Wegener cited both geological and biological evidence in support of his explanation. Similar plant and animal fossils are found in rock layers more than 200 million years old in those regions where he claimed that different continents were once aligned. Wegener attributed this to the migration of plants and animals freely throughout these broad regions. If 200 million years ago Africa and South America had been separated by the Atlantic Ocean as they are today, their climates, environments, and life forms should have been very different from each other—but they were not. Despite Wegener's use of evidence and logic to develop his explanations, other scientists found it difficult to imagine how solid, brittle continents could plow through the equally solid and brittle rock material of the ocean floor.

Wegener did not have an explanation for how the continents moved. Since there was no plausible mechanism for continental drift, the idea did not take hold. The hypothesis of continental drift was equivalent to the hypothesis of evolution in the decades before Darwin, when evolution lacked the idea of variation followed by natural selection as an explanatory mechanism. The argument essentially lay dormant until improved technologies allowed scientists to gather previously unobtainable data. From the mid 1950s through the early 1970s, new evidence for a mechanism to explain continental drift became available that the scientific community could accept.

Sonar mapping of the ocean floor revealed the presence of a winding, continuous ridge system around the globe. These ridges were places where molten material was welling up from the earth's interior and pushing apart the plates that form the earth's surface. In a relatively short time, these new observations, measurements, and interpretations provoked a complete shift in the thinking of the scientific community. Geologists now accept the idea that the surface of the earth is broken up into about a dozen large pieces, as well as a number of smaller ones, called tectonic plates. On a time scale of millions of years, these plates shift about on the planet's surface, changing the relative positions of the continents.

The plate tectonic model provides explanations that are widely accepted for the evolution of crustal features such as folded mountain chains, zones of active volcanoes and earthquakes, and deep ocean floor trenches. Direct measurements using the satellite-based global positioning system (GPS) to measure absolute longitude and latitude verify that the plates collide, move apart, and slide past one another in different areas along their adjacent boundaries at speeds comparable to the growth rate of a human fingernail.

In copying its DNA nucleotides, however, cells inevitably make a small number of mistakes. For this reason, a few nucleotides are changed through random error each time that a cell divides. (For example, an A in the DNA sequence of a gene in a chromosome may be replaced with a G in the new copy made as the cell divides.) Therefore, the larger number of cell divisions that have elapsed between the time that two organisms diverged from their common ancestor, the more differences there will be in their DNA sequences due to chance errors. This molecular divergence allows researchers to track evolutionary events by sequencing the DNA of different organisms.

For example, the lineage that led to humans and to chimpanzees diverged about 5 million years ago—whereas one needs to look back in time about 80 million years to find the last common ancestor shared by mice and humans. As a result, there is a much smaller difference between human and chimpanzee DNA than between human (or chimpanzee) and mouse DNA. In fact, scientists today routinely use the differences they can measure between the DNA sequences of organisms as "molecular clocks" to decipher the relationships between living things. The same comparisons among organisms can be made using the proteins encoded by DNA. For example, every living cell uses a protein called cytochrome c in its energy metabolism.

The cytochrome c proteins from humans and chimpanzees are identical. But there is only an 86 percent overlap in the molecules between humans and rattlesnakes, and only a 58 percent overlap between us and brewer's yeast. This is explained by the evolutionary proposition that we shared a common ancestor with chimps relatively recently, whereas the common ancestor that we, as vertebrates, shared with rattlesnakes is much more ancient. Still farther in the past, we and yeast shared a common ancestor—and the molecular data reflect this pattern. In the past few decades, new methods have been developed that are allowing us to obtain the exact sequence of all of the DNA nucleotides in chromosomes.

The Human Genome Project, for example, will produce when completed the entire sequence of the 3 billion nucleotides that make up our genetic inheritance. The complete sequence of the yeast genome (12 million nucleotides) is already known, as are the genomes for numerous species of bacteria. Similar sequencing efforts will soon yield the complete sequences for hundreds of bacteria and other organisms with small genomes. These molecular studies are powerful evidence for evolution. The exact order of the genes on our chromosomes can be used to predict the order on monkey or even mouse chromosomes, since long stretches of the chromosomes of mammalian species are so similar.

Even the parts of our DNA that do not code for proteins and at this point have no known function are similar to the comparable parts of DNA in related organisms. The confirmation of Darwin's ideas about "descent with modification" by this recent molecular evidence has been one of the most exciting developments in biology in this century. In fact, as the chromosomes of more and more organisms are sequenced over the next few decades, these data will be used to reconstruct much of the missing history of life on earth—thereby compensating for many of the gaps that still remain in the fossil record.

7

Contemporary Issues in Teacher Training

Biology is central to the dual challenge since many of the greatest personal and societal decisions of the future will involve health, the environment, and agriculture. Coupledwith the visibility and centrality of biology is the rapid generation of new knowledge in the field. Biology teachers confront a swiftly evolving discipline that presents both exhilarating opportunity and a sometimes overwhelming flow of new information, techniques, and applications. The last decade has brought genetic engineering, molecular forensics, biodiversity, and infectious disease to the public eye.

Most biology teachers have scrambled to incorporate new topics and illustrations into their courses to keep them current and lively. But we need to prepare our students to integrate and evaluate advances in science and technology after they leave our courses as well. To help nonmajors become literate in biology and to educate the new generation of biologists, teachers at the college level need a variety of well-tested tools and approaches to teaching and learning.

We need to train students in the process of analysis and critical thinking so they can successfully face the deluge of information, decisions, and problems they will be confronted with in life or in careers as biologists. Introductory courses in biology provide a critical forum for addressing the dual challenge. It is in these courses that teacher can excite students about careers in biology or turn them off to further training in science; it is also in these courses that we have an opportunity (often the *only* opportunity) to convince non-science majors that they are capable of thinking about scientific information and ideas.

Biology teachers are supported in the goal to involve students actively in science by a national mandate. Many influential entities in science policy have advocated taking the steps necessary to create a scientifically literate public and to attract more people to careers in science through promotion of active learning in the science classroom. Exciting times lie ahead. The reform of science education is challenging, but innovative teachers are receiving enthusiastic support from funding agencies, the government, and the public. Most importantly, the rewards for introducing students to the exhilaration of scientific discovery are well worth the effort. If we are to make our students truly scientifically literate, we should invite them to participate in the process of doing science.

If our invitation is to be credible, it must be issued in an environment that is supportive, cooperative and inclusive. Therefore, we need to incorporate into our classrooms the process of scientific inquiry, not just the information resulting from it, and learn how to construct classroom cultures that foster mutual respect and seek active participation from every member. Engaging students in the process of scientific investigation and the intellectual debate that accompanies it requires a classroom culture that motivates learning, teaches analytical skills as well as information, and captures the spirit of curiosity and questioning. This can be accomplished by building a classroom community.

Students may initially resist active learning in biology classes. Many of them enter biology courses believing they should be passive receptacles for information because they have nothing to offer biology. It is our challenge as teachers to convince all students that they can be active, contributing members of the community of biologists in the classroom. To overcome their passivity, we need to provide students with a supportive environment that encourages them to take an active role. Students who feel accepted and valued as members of a community will take responsibility for their own learning. If their initial attempts to contribute ideas are treated with respect, they will contribute again. Before long, they will be hooked on the fun and excitement of participating in a community of biologists – debating, hypothesising, and learning.

You may hesitate at the thought of challenging your students to be active members of the classroom community. Perhaps you feel you have had little experience in managing an active class or worry about losing control of the class. But the rewards of active learning are immediately evident for the teacher as well as the student. The joy of teaching in a classroom community is in watching the students discover the true excitement of biology and become sophisticated thinkers, exchanging ideas with one another. Just as biologists learn from each other, developing, refining, and challenging ideas cooperatively, so students learn from and with each other.

Furthermore, students learn complex thinking skills – problem-solving, divergent thinking, critical analysis – better in cooperative groups than individually or competitively. A major barrier to teaching and learning biology is that some students lack the necessary skills for learning in science courses.

To be successful in achieving scientific literacy for a diversity of students, we must directly face the inadequacy of our educational system in teaching the practical skills or fostering the confidence and independence needed for learning science. Bright, competent students who are successful in humanities courses often express frustration at their inability to master material, extract key concepts, or prepare for exams in their science courses. An understanding of the skills and attitudes needed to learn science can improve our teaching and help our students develop better strategies for learning.

A democratic society needs scientifically literate citizens of diverse ethnicity, gender, and culture, and class. The future will demand the citizenry to have more scientific knowledge to be involved in decisions that affect human health and the health of the environment. But in the past, science has not attracted all people in proportion to their representation in the general population. Since the inception of education, women and ethnic minorities have been underrepresented in science, and this situation continues today. Science needs diverse scientists to remain vigorous and dynamic. In every field of science, in every era, there have been great scientists who did not resemble their contemporaries either in personal or intellectual traits.

The leaders in science are those who are not trapped by current dogma or conventions, but instead bring a different perspective or approach to old problems. Progress in science depends on people such as Einstein, Galileo, Mendel, or McClintock, who have uncommon ideas and the confidence to pursue them. And yet, due to budget constraints and tradition, our educational system rigorously selects for scientist who, like many of their members, can perform well in a completive environment, on multiple choice exams, and who can absorb and memorise countless facts and not change the status quo.

To meet our responsibility to generate a scientifically literate citizenry and to attract a wider range of human types to science, we need to construct an educational system that accommodates and encourages people who do not fit the current mold of the scientist. We need to provide an environment in which people who reject competition as part of learning can flourish, an atmosphere that stimulates individuality, creativity, and curiosity. Most importantly, we need to accommodate various learning styles. In classrooms that are genuinely inclusive, students who see systems in their entirety should be as successful as their classmates who see the component parts.

Those who prefer intuition should find a place alongside the deductive reasoners. Meeting the needs of diverse students is facilitated by diverse teaching methods. Many methods may enhance learning, but some are particularly well-adapted to teaching biology. Incorporating cooperative learning and open-ended investigation into traditional classrooms may help the non-traditional student find a place in science and can enhance the creativity and problem-solving ability of the science major. Furthermore, we can teach students to appreciate their own learning styles to help them become informed and self-aware, thereby taking an essential step toward becoming successful learners.

Teaching Cellbiology

Traditional science laboratories have served many pedagogic functions. Some are used for reenforcing materials covered in lecture or the text. They are simply adjunct resources for the presentation of additional facts. The lab is typically content oriented and is known familiarly as a "cookbook" procedure. The labs are time and place dependent, but cost efficient and effective for their purpose. They are also useful for large enrollment classes since they require little or no alteration between multiple sections of lab. Nearly everyone who has had a "classical" botany or zoology lab or unfortunately, most general biology labs, has experienced this approach. Alternatively, laboratories can be inquiry based, research based or problem-oriented.

Inquiry labs attempt to balance content with concept and are more open-ended. The student is directed to ask a series of questions or is given a series of questions to answer. The answers and/or outcomes are unknown to the student, but known to the instructor. Good lab design leads the student to the "correct" conclusions generally pre-determined by the instructor. This lab approach remains time and place dependent but attempts to engage the student in a more personal approach. Early attempts at computer assisted instruction were based on reducing the time and place dependency of this model, with the added advantage of individual processing by the student.

A highly effective model of inquiry based learning was the BSCS programme of the 1960's. The literature abounds with computer modeling and simulations. Research labs take the inquiry one step further and ask questions that do not have pre-determined answers. This model engages students in "real science" where the outcome is unknown, at least in all of its details. Learning is highly individual and usually requires the development of sophisticated laboratory skills. It also requires more instructor time and expertise. Consequently, projects usually reflect the research interest of the instructor and the facilities of the institution.

This is an expensive approach to lab. It requires considerable time and materials and is based on the older apprentice model of education.

It is usually reserved for the best of the majors and is rarely used in lower division courses with large numbers of students. It is difficult to schedule, and is highly dependent on place. Often, research projects require a significant investment in facilities and support staff and most projects are done within the facilities of the faculty supervisor. The latest vogue in science education is problemoriented learning. This is a modification of a research plan and involves new problems for the student, but not necessarily for the instructor. Labs are learner focused, cooperative team efforts, with a high level of "ownership."

All knowledge is contextual and students learn only what they need to solve a problem. Case studies are often employed for starting points and the outcome is flexible but usually able to be controlled. The instructor's role is to choose appropriate case studies and attempt to steer the process in a particular direction (often to ensure content coverage). This approach to lab requires extensive library holdings and often-sophisticated facilities. It is also more demanding of instructor time in the role of facilitator. So, which is best. For us, the answer is a combination of all of the above with a focus on how real problems are solved in science. None of the strategies mentioned above are appropriate to the way science is actually done.

Each approach highlights only one aspect of solving a problem. For most laboratory scientists, the process of solving a problem is likely to begin with the recognition of an interesting question or topic. Sometimes this can be assigned by others, but more likely, it is a phenomenon that grabs our attention and one for which we don't have adequate easy answers. Once the problem is formulated, the next step is invariably checking the literature. The equivalent today would be to run it through a search engine on your browser. One need to know what has been reported before one can ask intelligent questions.

Having gained enough knowledge from the literature about the topic, we feel easier about approaching our peers. If the experts don't have a satisfactory solution, our interests may get piqued even more and then the fun begins. We decide to find a solution through experimentation. There is a problem or question that no one seems to have an acceptable answer. We first design a protocol based on our experience and skill and often expand those skills as it becomes necessary. Take, for example, a problem dealing with genetic variability. It could easily lead us to learn new techniques of molecular biology (PCR, restriction mapping, sequencing), while leading us away from the familiar and comfortable (microscopy, histology, karyotypes).

We discover that while every technique has merit to someone, only a few will be relevant to a given problem. And some are more relevant than others. If we are going to answer a problem, we learn the techniques that are required. Alternatively, one learns a technique and then never asks questions that can not be answered with that technique. The typical cell biology lab teaches techniques. Some will be used at a later date, most will not. Even twenty years ago, questions of genetic code would have been quite limited by the techniques available for RNA/DNA studies, when compared to modern procedures.

Today, we are making digital videos of the movement of SNRPs within a nucleus, and publishing it on the Internet. Consequently, it is time to evaluate, once again, our laboratory approach to cell biology. Instead of a traditional syllabus of 12-14 weeks with each week devoted to a different technique, the focus of the lab should be a project aimed at the solution of a problem. Rather than begin the sequence with "How to use a microscope," we should lay out a number of case studies, appropriate problems, or better still, use the first weeks to focus on teaching our students how to spot a significant problem that can be addressed. This is best done by utilising group projects that require constant interaction and focus.

Each group must be able to state the problem with sufficient clarity that all members of the group understand what is being asked and find their role within the solution. The main role of the instructor is to elicit the ideas, help to refine them and keep them on track. It is also important that the problems are stated in terms that are approachable in the limited time of a semester and with the equipment and facilities at hand.

For example, a student may wish to complete the genome sequence for Arabidopsis. With coaching and discussion, that may be whittled to using FISH to study the location and regulation of a single gene. That gene should be one for which there is a commercial source of an appropriate oligonucleotide for the hybridization. At this point, students begin to group themselves around the basic ideas and some are accepted as appropriate while others are left open for further work. Then the groups must decide what is it that they need to know before proceeding.

In the example above, the students would have to determine what FISH is (fluorescent in situ hybridization) and how it applies to visualising the action of a gene. There is no better way to determine this then using the web. Simple searches of "genome and localisation" will yield a host of appropriate papers and abstracts, some of which will refer to visualising the process. Then, the students ask for a review of FISH. If it is appropriate the instructor may choose to give a 20 minute or 3 hour lecture, or better, ask an expert to give a seminar to the group, or visit a laboratory where it is being performed.

In other circumstances the students will do a review of the procedure and report it to the group. The important part is that FISH is introduced as a means of solving a question and not as an isolated technique. If they do not need to use FISH, it may never be covered in the course. The protocols are selected on the basis of the stated problems and often come from on-line sources. Since this is a course on advanced cell imaging techniques, there are some basics. All aspects of microscopy are covered to some extent, usually by careful selection of the projects.

Standard light, dark field and phase microscopy, photomicrography, and fluorescence are covered. If appropriate, TEM, SEM and AFM might be covered, at least in principle. All students are introduced to digital and analog techniques of image recording, including the use of scanners, darkroom techniques and file formats. All projects must utilise some form of image processing and analysis. The specifics are left to the students, but in our experience, Adobe Photoshop-and/or Corel Photopaint-work well for most image manipulations. These are PC based programmes, but students opt for similar programmes for Macintosh or even UNIX based programmes.

Metamorph-is used for advanced work (including 3D deconvolution) although NIH Image? and/or Sigma Scan-are also employed. Digital video and morphing are introduced and 3D reconstruction is accomplished with Spyglass Slicer-(now NOeSYS?). All projects are eventually published on the web and each student creates a home page. There are now so many programmes for this that the students invariably lead the way. As a start they are introduced to the UNIX system on campus and learn to FTP and Pico edit from the start. Now for the best part.

Most of the images needed are available on the web. It is not necessary for a student to know how to do FISH if the images they need can be obtained from elsewhere. They should understand what the procedure is, but do not need to be skilled at performance of a protocol. For undergraduate projects, there is an almost unlimited resource of images available on the net. Normally, our projects are focused on protocols that can be performed by students, but they know from the start that it is the analysis that is important.

For example, one of last year's projects involved the reconstruction of a chloroplast. The project centered on the relationship of a glyoxysome to the chloroplast when it was noted that published images were always 2D TEMs. Without realising what a formidable task lay ahead, the students chose to obtain serial sections of a chloroplast, digitise the images, stack them and reconstruct a rotatable image (hopefully in relation to microbodies in the cytoplasm). This was not a trivial undertaking, since cutting serial sections requires quite a lot of skill.

Fortified with the enthusiasm of ignorance but excited about the ultimate image the students forged ahead. What they found was a citation that gave a series of 2D images of a sectioned plant cell. When photocopied and faxed images proved too blurry, they contacted the author by email, explained their project and obtained a set of original photomicrographs (by snail mail). The author was not up to the task of creating the digital images and was surprised by the students' request for images that they could receive by FTP. The project was completed with the supplied images, even though the students, as a back-up, had fixed and embedded plant materials and learned to use a TEM.

The images merely saved them many hours of sectioning and allowed them to put their time into the 3D reconstruction. As for the relation to the glyoxysome, the students learned that it was not as easy a solution as they had originally thought. They have a new respect for the published work of others. The basic procedure is:

- Find a topic that excites the student curiosity
- Search the literature (web browsers, search engines) and refine the problem
- Obtain published images (FTP or download from the net)
- Digitise and enhance images (threshold, erase unwanted material)
- Image Analysis (counts, area, crosssection diameter, etc.)
- Morph or 3D reconstruction
- Plan and execute presentation on home page or as Authorware presentation.

Our focus is on an image as data. It matters how the image was obtained, but the real work begins with the image. The production of a visual answer to a problem of interest to the student leads to retention of more content than one would imagine. The students become creative with their work and are justly proud of their accomplishment. Equally important, they learn to work with a team toward a set deadline. They do not waste time going over cookbook protocols and techniques they may never use. Finally, they come to realise that they can either master any technique if there is a need for it or find someone who is a master to cooperate.

Models and Games

Cell biology is far from having an adequate pedagogy to introduce students into the explosive new concepts of modern biology. A simple survey in reference data base banks indicate that while for the key-word "cell" more than a 100,000 references can be found per year, when key-words "cell" and "education" or "cell biology" and "education" are searched together only about 100 or 10 references are found, respectively.

As producers of basic cell biology knowledge in a third world country, we feel engaged into the challenge of science popularisation in our own field of investigation and in creating tools for school and science museums activities that could contribute to decrease this gap between science and society. A first set of activities were developed and conduced from 1983 until 1987 with a group of scientists that founded in Rio de Janeiro the "Espaço Ciência Viva" (Space for a living science).It was original to get microscopes in public squares and favelas in Rio, and a co-operation with local community associations allowed a perfect integration of the activities with social events organised for special and thematic science affairs called as "Day of the cell" or "Day of the water" or "Night of the sky".

Young and old people were allowed to manipulate microscopes to see some previously made preparations on different types of cells, or even their own slide preparations made locally, and to observe, to draw what was seen, to talk about, learn, play or just have fun. Such activities in the public squares were always conjugated to a trip inside a cell, that was introduced with a lecture upon slide presentation of optical and electron microscope images, and that soon showed a low power of communication, since scales for the microcosmos are completely unknown for the general public.

The same microscope images were then used for the construction of different cell models. In 1988 a first giant cell model was set up for the I Congress of Biotechnology and then exposed in the science museum place of Espaço Ciência Viva. In 1999 a new giant model was set up in the Life Museum at FIOCRUZ. Plant cell transmission and scanning electron microscopy micrographs were obtained to present structural details such as the cell wall, cellulose fibrils, plasma membrane, the nucleus, nuclear membrane, chromatin material, the Golgi apparatus, the endoplasmic reticulum, ribosomes, mitochondria, chloroplasts, microtubule networks and vacuoles.

Modelling was made as close as possible from the original images, that are most commonly different from draws that are found in textbooks. In the two museums, the giant model were integrated with experiments with microscopes that allow observation of micro-organisms, cell diversity and reconstruction of the cell theory, with photo panels for re-discovering cell model details in parallel with the original images from which the model was generated. Microscopes coupled to video allow observation of cell movements and fecundating.

Games and multimidia CD-ROMs do support more information and fun on the history of microscopy and of the cell theory, the visualisation of a larger number of cell images. The intense empathy of children and adults while entering inside the giant cell model pushed us to develop more models and games using microscopic cell images as starting points. Lymphocyte and neurone models were obtained using latex balloons filled with water, in an activity were the relative size of the different organelles was not so strictly obtained but where gel/water consistency of the cell, and their main compartments can be perceived by the students and the general public.

Vegetal cells that can be observed in the optical microscope focusing on leaves of the aquatic plant *Elodea* were used to prepare optical and electron microscopy images from which 3-D models were generated by scaling increases of 10, 40 or 100 thousand times, maintaining the relative size of each cell organelle. Besides the models, that can be more or less interactive depending on the way an activity with them is presented, the development of games leading children to play with cells is another objective of our investigations. Cellulose transparency sheets were used to reproduce optical and electron microscopy that served for plastic moulding of different organelles and relative volumetric filling on the cytoplasm.

A puzzle ("The cell puzzle") was develop upon optical microscope images at different magnifications, in which the goal is to assemble the individual pieces that are not cut aleatory but at the real boundaries defined by cell wall, then reconstructing the original tissue with individual cells. Another game, called "The cell investigator" challenges the participants to go through a tray representing the cell cytoplam, and to solve a case (e.g. the membrane case, or the mitochondria case) in which a question has to be answered by reasoning after collecting and assembling disperse information that can be obtained in cards throughout the different compartments disposed in the tray.

The cards report images, experiment results, comments, tables, histories and if appropriate reasoning is made, the participant will elucidate and solve the case, just as scientists do (or secret agents do). These initiatives are now integrated in three different fronts of interchange between scientists and society:

(1) museum exhibition and activities during school visits, and

(2) testing of prototypes of the games with teachers directly with their students in classrooms of different levels, and

(3) inserting the practice of creating new games and models as an activity in courses and workshops designed for the training of school teachers.

Web-based Simulations

The Biology Lab On-Line Project is a component of the California State University System (CSU) Integrated Technology Strategy (ITS), which calls for anywhere, anytime access to information. The project initially brought together biologists from throughout the CSU system and the CSU Center for Distributed Learning (CDL) to explore ways to use technology to improve learning in introductory biology laboratories. Later, multimedia developers from Addison Wesley Longman were added to the development team. A major goal of the collaboration was to allow students to learn as biologists do, *i.e.*, by actively designing experiments and interpreting their results.

Another goal was to extend student learning opportunities by creating simulations of experiments that they might not normally do because of expensive and/or inaccessible lab equipment, lack of field opportunities, time constraints, complexity, danger, or ethical problems. Eliminating the time constraints of the traditional experiment and two or three hour laboratory period gives students the opportunity to design and interpret experiments, learn from their mistakes, and to revise and redo their experiments just like real scientists.

The simulations are not designed to replace the traditional "wet labs" found in the normal biology course, but rather are designed to extend the laboratory experience to subjects and experiments that can not normally be done, or not done enough, in a traditional laboratory. The simulations are also *not* multi-media presentations, stand-alone tutorials or on-line courses. The project has produced five different educational simulations covering the subjects of evolution, Mendelian genetics, protein translation, human population demography, and protein structure-function. Current projects in progress and due to be finished by the summer of 1999 will simulate human genetics, mitochondrial electron transport, glycolysis, human female reproductive physiology, and photosynthesis. While each of the simulations is unique, all of them share many common interface elements and functions.

All of the simulations have been designed so that the student can carry out many different experiments, allowing the student to design and interpret their own experiments. The flexibility of the programmes make well designed exercises an important part of each laboratory. However, while sample exercises will be included with each lab, instructors can easily design their own exercises to meet the needs of their students. The simulations have all been created in the Java programming language, so that they can be easily accessed over the web using any standard browser. This solves the problem of widely disseminating the applications, a common problem with most educational software.

The Java application provides the user interface where students set the starting parameters for their experiment and get graphical feedback on their current settings. In some of the simulations the Java programme also calculates the results, while in others the input parameters are passed back to the server, where the real calculations take place. When the server is done it sends the results back to the Java application, which presents the results to the student. The downside of using Java is that only individuals and schools with fairly new computers and software (Netscape 3 or better, etc.) and an internet connection can use the software.

Another disadvantage of using Java is the inability of Java programmes to save to disk or print. This limitation has been overcome through the use of a notebook that can be exported to a web page. All of the data tables, such as numbers of different types of progeny, or results of statistical calculations, can be imported directly into the notebook. After typing in their comments the student can export the notebook to a web page for printing, or to email to themselves or an instructor. The web page is temporarily stored on the server. Graphical images such as graphs and charts produced by some of the programmes are also exportable to the notebook, where they can then be printed. All of the programmes share some common user interface elements, including a title bar with links to an introduction to the lab, help, sample assignments, the notebook, etc.

While there is much diversity in how the different labs operate, most of them start in an input mode where the student designs their experiment by adjusting different parameters. After designing the experiment the student runs the simulation. The programme calculates the results of the experiment, usually in a minute or less, and then presents the results in the output mode. In this mode there is a tabbed interface where the student chooses which type of output they wish to view, a table of the data, a graph, the input values, etc. After analysing their results they can import them into the notebook and then go back to the input mode to design another experiment. This ability to quickly go back and forth between the design of an experiment and the results is one of the powerful advantages of a simulation approach to teaching science.

EvolveIT

Although evolution is the unifying theme of the biological sciences, it is perhaps one of the most misunderstood and difficult concepts to convey in a laboratory setting. The study of evolution is especially suited to computer simulations because evolution normally occurs over very long time intervals, large data sets are usually needed to understand it, and there are usually a number of important parameters that are difficult to control in real experiments. EvolveIT, is a web based, interactive computer simulation designed to teach the basic concepts of natural selection and to convey the importance of time in the evolutionary process. Students using EvolveIT observe evolutionary changes in bird beak morphology in hypothetical populations of birds isolated on two islands.

In the simulation students can set the annual rainfall on island(s) containing finch populations, and then observe the effect of this environment on the evolution of the finch's beaks. Students may also change several other properties of the bird populations, such as initial mean beak size, beak size variability, beak size heritability and mean clutch size, to determine their effect on beak evolution. To help students clearly see the effects of changes in the different variables, the simulation uses two islands with independent and isolated populations. A student can either directly compare two different sets of conditions, or do a duplicate run where both populations have identical starting conditions.

As many students will also be unfamiliar with some of the variables, the programme gives extensive feedback on what is being changed with each alteration of one of the initial variables. For instance, when the slider for mean beak size is moved to the right a picture of a finch head shows the finch beak growing larger, or when variability is increased a graph of the current distribution of beak sizes spreads out. The programme creates several hundred different virtual "birds" using the initial parameters entered by the student. These birds then go through a round of natural selection where each bird's probability of survival is a function of the seed distribution (determined by the setting for rainfall) and that bird's beak size.

After the selection step the surviving birds are randomly mated to one another. They then produce offspring based on the values for heritability and variability entered by the student. This new population of birds becomes the starting population for the next year. This repeats for each year of the simulation. Because of the random selection and mating each simulation run is unique and will produce a different result than any other run, even one that starts with exactly the same starting parameters. The programme produces several different outputs: a scrolling table with the mean beak size, the variability and the population size for every year of the simulation, for both populations; a series of histograms showing what proportion of birds of different beak sizes survived, for each year of the simulation; a plot of the mean beak size versus time for both populations; and a plot of the population size versus time for both populations.

The final output is a table with the initial values for the simulation. The student can rerun the simulation with the same initial values, revise the experiment, or start over with the default values and design a new experiment. Students can study the effects of different amounts of rainfall on the evolution of beak size to get a feel for how natural selection works. They should be able to determine that large beaks are favored in low rainfall, the optimum beak size for different amounts of rainfall, the effect of varying the severity of the selection, and the importance of the environment in determining the direction of selection. Similar experiments can be done in which only population variability or beak size heritability is manipulated to study how these parameters affect beak evolution.

Changes in island size affect the carrying capacity of the island and allow the student to investigate the stochastic effects that can result from small population size. Variations in clutch size permit the student to investigate the consequences of different fecundities on the capacity of different species to evolve. Some aspects of population dynamics can also be investigated using this parameter (rate of exponential growth, boom bust population cycles, etc.) While the simulation is based on Darwin's finches, changes in the species variables such as mean beak size, variability, heritability and clutch size create virtual species that can have properties similar to many other wild species.

Students can investigate the parameters that are more likely to lead to the extinction of endangered species, see why some species might evolve faster than others, and examine many other facets of evolution. The programme generates large data sets, one run can produce 600 data points, so students can learn how to analyse and interpret large amounts of data, unlike the situation in a typical lab. The great flexibility of the programme should allow individual instructors to tailor student assignments to their particular preferences and provide students with a real opportunity to design their own experiments. Actively engaging students in exploring and studying evolution through this simulation will provide another avenue for students to learn about evolution in addition to the traditional text and lecture explanations.

Virtual Fly Lab

Two genetics labs are currently planned. One is a simulation of classical fruit fly genetics while the other one lets the student study human genetics by analysing pedigrees. The Virtual Fly Lab simulation is an update to the Virtual Fly Lab originally created by Bob Desharnais. In the Virtual Fly Lab students design their own fruit flies by choosing from many different possible phenotypes for characteristics such as eye color, wing shape, body color, etc. They then mate their flies and analyse the progeny to determine the rules of inheritance for different traits. Each experiment is unique and students can have up to 10,000 progeny produced from one mating. Offspring can also be mated so a wide range of different experiments are possible.

There are 29 different traits that can be studied in isolation or in various combinations so the number of possible experiments is in the millions. The traits are all represented graphically so the student can observe the phenotypes directly. For instance, if the student selects the white eye mutation for the female parent their picture of the female parent will change to have white eyes. After the mating they will get a picture of the different progeny, along with numbers beside each picture to indicate the number of progeny of that type (number of females with white eyes, females with red eyes, etc.) The programme includes a Chi Square calculator for doing statistical tests of the students hypotheses, and a notebook for recording results, observations, hypotheses and conclusions.

Students can import the numerical results from their crosses and statistical tests directly into the notebook. Using this programme students can discover or study most of the important principles of Mendelian genetics, including dominant and recessive alleles, sex-linkage, lethal alleles, independent assortment, epistasis, linkage, gene order, linkage groups, and linkage maps. More importantly, students can discover these principles by doing the same sort of experiments as the original researchers, only much faster. The programme is appropriate for a wide range of biology courses as the assignment determines the level of difficulty. Students can do statistical tests, but this is not required.

Students can do complicated crosses with multiple traits, or simple crosses with only one trait at a time. If a student is confused by a complicated cross, they can always do some additional simpler crosses to try to figure out what is going on. They can also do additional crosses with the progeny from their crosses, and their progeny, etc. This ability to devise their own experiments and try many different permutations is a major strength of the FlyLab.

PedigreeLab

PedigreeLab will generate numerous pedigrees for a particular genetic disease. The student can examine the pedigrees to determine the inheritance pattern of the particular disease. In addition, the student will be able to examine various molecular markers and determine whether they are linked to the genetic disease. This is a key process in the current search for human genetic disease genes and is normally very difficult to explain to students. Having them actually go through the process should significantly improve their learning of these difficult concepts.

TranslateIT

So far, the Biolabs project has produced two molecular biology simulations. The first, TranslateIT, simulates some of the original experiments used to crack the genetic code, one of the key discoveries in molecular biology. These experiments rely on radioactive materials and difficult to produce RNA templates so they can't be done in the normal biology lab. Students design and create simple RNA molecules in the simulation that they then translate in a virtual *in vitro* translation mix. The programme shows a simple animation of the techniques that would be used to analyse the products of the translation and then gives them the amino acid sequence of any proteins produced in their experiment.

The student must logically analyse the results of multiple experiments to deduce the properties of the genetic code, just as the original researchers did, only with the advantage of being able to do experiments in minutes that normally take months to carry out. Various properties of the code that can be determined using this simulation are the triplet nature of the code, that the code is non-overlapping, codon assignments for particular amino acids, and the existence and identity of stop codons.

HemoglobinLab

In the second molecular biology simulation, the HemoglobinLab, students investigate various aspects of the molecular biology of hemoglobin, using case studies. The goal is for the student to learn how changes in the nucleotide sequence of a gene *may* effect the protein sequence, which *may* effect the structure of the protein, which *may* effect the function of the protein, which *may* effect the properties of the cell, which *may* in turn effect the physiology of the individual.

Students choose a case by selecting a patient from a pull down menu with a list of over a dozen patients. For each case the students can examine the doctors notes about the symptoms and medical history of the patient, examine the color of a vial of the patients blood, examine the blood under a microscope to see if there are changes in the red blood cells, run a sample of the blood on an electrophoresis gel to determine if there are physical changes in the globin protein, and, finally, the student can determine the amino acid sequence of the patients globin protein.

Having determined the sequence of the protein the student can go to the DNA sequence editor and try to alter the DNA sequence of the normal gene to see what type of DNA mutation would cause the changes found in the patient they are examining. The patients have a variety of mutations in the globin gene ranging from simple point mutations that change one amino acid, such as in sickle cell anemia, to deletions and insertions causing frameshifts, such as some of the thallasemias. The mutations cause many different patient phenotypes, such as anemia, brown blood, polycythemia (too many red blood cells), and purple skin color.

DemographyLab

The DemographyLab, models human population growth in several different countries around the world. Students can use this lab to investigate how differences in population size, age-structure, and age-specific fertility and mortality rates affect human population growth. Default values for seven countries have been incorporated into the programme to allow comparisons between nations with very different demographics, such as Japan and Nigeria. In addition, students can change any of the parameters to create their own experiments.

The proportion of males and females in each five year age group, the total population size, the mortality rate for males and females in each five year age group and the birth rate per female in each five year age group can all be set by the student using a simple graphical interface. After running the simulation for 100, 200 or 300 years, students get summary statistics for the population at the end of the time interval, such as life expectancy, birth rate, population growth rate, etc. They can view a line graph of population numbers over the course of their experiment, see a graphical representation of the population structure for every five years of the experiment, or examine the number of males and females in each age group for each five year period. Using the programme a variety of demographic phenomena can be demonstrated, such as exponential growth and decline, stable age structure, zero population growth, demographic momentum, dependency ratios, sex ratios and marriage squeezes.

MitochondriaLab

Three biochemistry and cell biology labs currently in development are MitochondriaLab, GlycolysisLab, and PlantLab. MitochondriaLab will simulate electron transport, proton gradients and oxidative phosphorylation in mitochondria. Students will be able to recreate the classic experiments that established the chemiosmotic theory as the mechanism for energy production in the cell. They will add various substrates and inhibitors to their virtual mitochondrial extracts and then measure the consumption of oxygen over time. From their results they can work out some of the steps in the pathway and the mechanism by which the chemical energy is converted into ATP molecules.

GlycolysisLab

In GlycolysisLab students will study the enzymatic reactions of the glycolysis pathway and the kinetics of biochemical reactions by varying quantities of substrates and cofactors and then measuring reaction rates.

PlantLab

The PlantLab will simulate the photosynthetic reactions in leaves. Students will vary wavelength and intensity of light, CO_2 and oxygen concentrations, temperature, etc. and then measure the consumption of CO_2 and the production of sugar in their simulated leaves.

ReproductionLab

The tenth and last lab currently under development is ReproductionLab. This lab will simulate the human female reproductive cycle. Students will be able to inject various hormones, alter diet and exercise, and remove organs in their virtual subjects and then can track hormonal changes and various physiological responses over time. Student experiments should lead to a greater understanding of hormone action, positive and negative feedback loops, homeostasis, reproductive cycles and physiological pathways. Understanding this physiological cycle is obviously of great importance to the students and will also teach them many important physiological concepts.

Bioinformatics

Bioinformatics plays a key role for science students

pursuing higher education. Roughly, bioinformatics describes any use of computers to handle biological information. In addition to its immediate value in the high school classroom, many students will likely benefit from an introduction to bioinformatics if they intend to pursue higher studies in bioscience disciplines such as:

- computational molecular biology, where computers are used to characterise the molecular components of living things
- comparative genomics, that looks for the differences and similarities in the genes of species
- structural genomics, i.e., identifying and predicting protein structures
- medical informatics, the management of biomedical data
- pharmacogenomics, that aims to identify drug targets by applying genomic approaches and technologies

Using bioinformatics can foster inquiry learning of content that has often been taught in a dry manner. The explosion of data produced by the Human Genome Project has called forth the creation of a new discipline—bioinformatics, whose focus is on the acquisition, storage, analysis, modeling, and distribution of the many types of information embedded in DNA and protein sequence data. The fundamental nature of science is imbedded in inquiry-based learning. Inquiry can be a very effective mechanism for better understanding the essence of science, its technical and reasoning processes, and the attitudes that accompany these processes.

Inquiry learning directly translates from the classroom to society as students search for answers to problems they have encountered in their home, school, or community. Using bioinformatic tools, students generate real data and more importantly apply these applications to independent problem solving. During this process they are actively engaged in the process of learning, and active learning strategies promote more effective learning. The U.S. National Science Education Standards (NSES) have provided guidelines to improve the learning environment. The standards have, in turn, yielded a widely endorsed set of specific goals, such as the following:

- Students should learn science and mathematics as active processes focused on a limited number of concepts.
- Curricula should stress understanding, reasoning, and problem solving rather than memorisation of facts, terminology, and algorithms.
- Teachers should engage students in meaningful activities that regularly and effectively employ calculators, computers, and other tools in the course of instruction.
- Bioinformatics will help teachers and students achieve these goals by providing opportunities to use new technologies during science activities.

Bioinformatics can provide the thread that connects many topics: protein structure, protein function, nucleic acids, genetics, genetic disease, evolution, cell biology, botany, and zoology. Most students view these topics as individual chapters in a book, unrelated to one another despite teachers' attempts to unify the material. Students study biochemistry, get their test grade, and then forget the material. Use of bioinformatics ties this information together while teaching analysis and interpretation skills in an active, productive learning environment. Integration of bioinformatics into the high school classroom will further advance biology education. "Technology makes learning more interactive, enjoyable, and customisable, and this improves students' attitudes toward the subject and their interest in learning."In addition, it can be argued that the introduction of this technology will prove to be an increasingly important aspect of science education.

Bioinformatics promotes the application of basic scientific research to the teaching of biology. These tools have been used in the classroom to demonstrate the importance of the primary structure in proteins, visualise the mechanism of translation from nucleic acid to protein, and teach about DNA sequencing, the Human Genome Project, and other topics that have previously left little room for student exploration. Learning of biotech issues and ethics can be augmented by bioinformatics. Bioinformatics supports the biotechnological techniques that are applied in the classroom. Certain techniques such as DNA fingerprinting and PCR are being used more and more frequently in high school classrooms, and can be facilitated by bioinformatics.

For example, if a class performs electrophoresis of the proteins in fish muscle, they can then go a step further and explore whether the actin found in both salmon and trout is identical or if there have been any evolutionary changes. Many current social and ethical controversies, such as genetic engineering biological warfare stem cell research as well as unsolved biological mysteries, such as the history of human evolution phylogenetic trees origins of species are raised by the students as they manipulate this data, thus leading to further explorations.

Utilising technology students can capitalise on these related explorations and thus exercise learner-control while increasing their motivation and making connections to the real world. Technology also allows for data-driven assessments tied to content standards that, when implemented systemically, enhance the achievement of students as measured in a variety of ways, including, but not exclusively limited to, standardised achievement tests."

8

Preparing Teachers for Biotechnology Classrooms

Nanotechnology Curriculum

The fundamental objective of nanotechnology is to model, simulate, design and manufacture nanostructures and nanodevices with extraordinary properties and assemble them economically into a working system with revolutionary functional abilities. Nanotechnology offers a new paradigm of groundbreaking material development by controlling and manipulating the fundamental building blocks of matter at nanoscale, that is, at the atomic/molecular level. Therefore, in order for our students to face the challenges presented by nanotechnology, the following educational goals should be applied:

– Provide understanding, characterisation and measurements of nanostructure properties

– Provide ability for synthesis, processing and manufacturing of nanocomponents and nanosystems

– Provide ability for design, analysis and simulation of nanostructures and nanodevices

– Prepare students to conduct research and development of economically feasible and innovative applications of nanodevices in all spheres of our daily life.

Nanotechnology should be taught by creating both knowledge-centered and learning-centered environments inside and outside the classroom. Because the technology is advancing so fast, activities that encourage creative thinking, critical thinking and life-long learning should be given the highest priority. Nanotechnology is truly interdisciplinary. An interdisciplinary curriculum that encompasses a broad understanding of basic sciences intertwined with engineering sciences and information sciences pertinent to nanotechnology is essential. Course design should incorporate science concepts from different fields. Other suggestions for teaching strategies include:

- Introductory nanotechnology courses should be taught more from the perspectives of concept development and qualitative analysis rather than mathematical derivations.
- Every effort should be made to convey the big picture and how different learning exercises fit together to achieve course objectives.
- Each course should be taught at the appropriate level with required pre-requisites.
- Junior and senior design courses, specifically the capstone design courses, should integrate modelling, simulation, control and optimisation of nanodevices and nanosystems into the course objectives.
- Every effort should be made to integrate concepts related to nanotechnology into all design courses.

Labs, research centres, educators, and mentors are key to hands-on learning. Interactive learning should be the hallmark of nanotechnology education. Technology can play a powerful role in facilitating interactive learning both inside and outside the classroom. Students should be given opportunities to work directly with established nanotechnology research centres to gain hands-on experience. University faculty members must collaborate with industry in order to educate and train students in the field of nanotechnology. Utilising a team of faculty members specialising in appropriate disciplines to teach nanotechnology courses is highly desirable.

Studying Biotechnology

Studying biotechnology can inspire students to study biology. To understand issues, students must learn the science behind the issues. Biotechnology can provide a "hook" for getting students interested in and excited about biology, since this topic is frequently featured in the news media illustrates the integration of basic scientific research into applied biology; for example, basic research about the biology of viruses that infect bacteria led to the modification of viral DNA to act as a vehicle for moving specific genes from one cell to another underlies many current social and ethical controversies encompasses methods that are widely used in all areas of biology, and students with an interest in biological research should be exposed to these techniques early in their training. In spite of the importance of biotechnology in modern biological science, many teachers are reluctant to include concepts about biotechnology in their classrooms because they are concerned that biotechnology:

- may be too complex for students
- may be too expensive to implement
- is not within the teacher's area of expertise
- may be too controversial to manage in the classroom.

However, many resources are available to help teachers incorporate laboratory and other biotechnology activities in the classroom, to provide background, and to facilitate discussions about controversial topics.

Biotechnology Methods

Modern biotechnology methods rely on the isolation and subsequent manipulation of DNA. Once students are familiar with DNA and its role in genetics, a useful starting point for introducing biotechnology concepts is DNA isolation.

Isolation of DNA

Although DNA isolation techniques vary slightly depending on the experimental organism, all of these techniques share the following characteristics:

- a treatment for breaking open cells and releasing DNA
- a method for removing or inactivating DNA-degrading enzymes
- a means of separating DNA from proteins and other contaminating molecules.

Transformation DNA

Another technique at the heart of many biotechnology methods, called DNA transformation, involves adding foreign DNA to cells. This foreign DNA then can be "turned on" to make a useful product. This method has been used to produce many pharmaceuticals, such as human insulin. For classroom purposes, DNA transformation is most easily accomplished in bacteria. The basic scheme is to

- take a bacterial mini-chromosome called a plasmid,

- insert foreign DNA into the plasmid,
- and then put the modified plasmid back into bacteria.

Many transformation laboratory exercises have been published. Some companies sell pre-packaged DNA transformation kits.

Restriction enzyme digestion and analysis

Restriction enzymes are proteins that cut DNA molecules at specific sequences of bases. These enzymes allow biotechnologists to reproducibly cut DNA molecules into well-defined fragments. Restriction enzymes are frequently used in biotechnology to analyse and make new DNA molecules. Typically, the analysis of DNA using restriction enzymes involves a technique called agarose gel electrophoresis. Agarose consists of chains of sugars, and has a consistency similar to gelatin when used for this purpose.

An electric current moves the DNA through the agarose, and the DNA molecules separate according to their size, with the smaller DNA molecules moving faster. Different-sized DNA bands can be analysed in a school lab. One of the easiest ways to incorporate these techniques in the classroom is to do a combined restriction enzyme digestion & agarose gel electrophoresis laboratory exercise. Typically, students would do a restriction enzyme digestion on an inexpensive, readily available DNA, then run that DNA in an agarose gel. Students would then analyse the pattern of different-sized DNA bands.

Polymerase chain reaction (PCR)

The PCR has become a common biotechnology technique for the production of multiple copies of relatively short

DNA molecules. This method is somewhat analogous to a molecular copy machine for pages (short sections) of DNA. PCR requires DNA that will act as a template short, single-stranded DNAs called primers (starting points for making DNA) an enzyme that makes DNA the building blocks of DNA called nucleotides a machine called a thermal cycler, which repeatedly subjects the reaction mixture to varying temperatures. Polymerase Chain Reaction can be demonstrated in the lab or by computer simulation.

There are a number of ways to incorporate PCR into the classroom. Simulations of PCR can enhance student understanding of the methodology without the need for equipment and supplies. Basic equipment, such as two or three water baths, can be used to perform the reactions if a thermal cycler is not available. For advanced classes, several exercises using a thermal cycler could be included. There are commercial pre-packaged kits for doing PCR in the classroom.

DNA Sequencing

DNA sequencing is the heart of the human genome project, and is indispensable for many biotechnology projects. The purpose of DNA sequencing is to determine the exact order of bases (letters) in a DNA molecule. This information can then inform a scientist about the nature of a protein encoded by that DNA, the likely evolutionary relationship between different organisms, and a wealth of other information. There are many avenues for incorporating DNA sequencing into the classroom. These include

- simulations done with pencil and paper
- downloading and analysing real sequence data over the internet

– having students prepare DNA (e.g., through PCR, as described above), sending out the DNA for sequencing, and then analysing the sequence data.

Microarrays

Until recently, when it came to answering questions like "Which genes are expressed in cancer cells that aren't expressed in normal cells?," a very laborious gene-by-gene analysis was required. Techniques using microarrays are now available.for simultaneously analysing the expression of many genes. These microarrays are made on either a glass slide or silicon chip, and contain hundreds or thousands of parts of genes in a small section of the slide or chip. In this procedure, the expressed genes are isolated from cells, after which those genes are detected by determining which DNAs on the chip bind to which genes from the cells. Wet lab exercises are difficult with this technology, since it is quite new and the supplies and equipment are expensive.

However, students can experience microarrays in several ways, including viewing examples of microarray data6 or viewing an internet-based simulation describing how gene expression is studied using microarrays. Many companies that manufacture microarrays have information for educators on their websites.

Ethical Issues

Biotechnology applications have generated many social and ethical controversies. In a biology classroom, The best approach is to help students understand the information behind developments in biotechnology so they can develop a fact-based understanding of the potential benefits and risks associated with these techniques. Some examples of biotechnology-based controversies include:

- genetically modified foods
- genetically engineering microbes for bioremediation
- cloning whole organisms
- embryonic stem cell research
- gene therapy
- genetic testing.

Scientists over decades have explored and mapped lands, oceans and the heavens with the expectation of increasing our awareness of the environment in which we live. Underlying this search for knowledge is also the desire to improve human existence through the discovery of beneficial resources. The Human Genome Project (HGP) has served to explore our genetic environment to make us aware of the beneficial resources that might contribute to understanding and improving our lives.

The HGP involves the discovery and sequence of the full DNA complement in a single human somatic cell. Its primary goal is a listing and location of our genes – the single unit of heredity responsible for how we develop from conception, how we grow and mature, how we live, and how we die. Dr. James Watson, one of the most well-known proponents of the Human Genome Project, contributed significantly along with Francis Crick, Rosalind Franklin and Maurice Wilkins to our understanding of the nature of DNA through the discovery of the structure of the DNA double helix. This discovery changed the focus of modern genetics and influenced the direction of many other disciplines in that the foundation of all life processes could now begin to be explored.

Since then, technological advances have enabled scientists to study DNA and its structure in detail.

Computer generated analysis tools designed specifically to understand the significance of the base sequence in this large macromolecule have aided the Human Genome Project tremendously. These tools also aid in understanding how biochemical processes encoded in the sequence of bases are maintained, controlled, duplicated and terminated. With the development and modernisation of the Fred Sanger dideoxy chain-terminating automatic sequencing method, the bacteria artificial chromosome (BAC) and the polymerase chain reaction (PCR), scientists have within 13 years been able to finish determining the order of 98% of the 3-billion nucleotide base pairs that compose the human genome. Simply knowing the sequence of bases at any given place or locus on a chromosome is not sufficient to understanding its function.

As important as the sequence is to the function of genes, their distribution, location and structure among the 23 chromosome pairs is just as valuable when determining their role in different life processes. The estimate of between 30,000 and 40,000 genes is based on the fact that exons (gene segments) within the genome are flanked by known marker sequences (e.g., splice sites) that are located along the linear DNA sequence. Some computer programmes can now recognise and label these segments and marker sequences while other programmes can predict the location and structures of genes in genomic sequences from a variety of organisms.

Through great effort and expense, scientists in molecular biology, biochemistry, math, computer science, engineering and the health care industry have worked together to turn what began in 1985 as a simple campus improvement project at the University of California, Santa Cruz into an international scientific consortium. This cooperative effort now known as the Human Genome Project, begun in 1989, was lead by the U.S. Department of Energy (DOE), formally the Atomic Energy Commission.

The DOE was charged to investigate genetic mutations and genome structural integrity after observing the consequences of the development of the atomic bomb. Many universities, private industries and non-profit organisations from around the world have worked together to produce a complete reconstruction of the human genome for public display. The institutions involved in this consortium are often referred to as "sequencing centres." These centres:

- offer facilities that allow scientists to determine the sequence of DNA of many different organisms including human
- spend time and money in disseminating sequence information into publicly accessible databases
- develop computer programmes that attempt to make biological sense out of the vast amount of sequence data being generated

The Internet has made it possible to gain instant access to DNA databases. The accelerated development of the Internet is due in no small part to the need for communication between scientists at various DNA sequencing centres and to provide public accessibility to a DNA sequence database initially set up at the National Institutes of Health (NIH) at National Center for Biotechnology Information (NCBI). The database called GenBank is the major warehouse of genome sequence information from many different species and is accessible from many other web sites devoted to the utilisation of sequence information. Technology accelerated the discovery of clues to heritable diseases and relationships among species.

April 25, 2003 marked 50 years since the publication in the journal Nature of the letter by James Watson and Francis Crick describing the DNA double helix structure. This day also marked the completion of the human genome sequence to 99.9% accuracy as announced by the National Human Genome Research Institute (NHGRI). In the wake of this enthusiasm for the completed project lies information that has only begun to provide science and medicine with clues to how to combat heritable diseases, how to improve medical applications, and how some of life's seemingly most insignificant organisms like the fly, roundworm and mouse give us clues to better understand our natural selves.

The door of discovery and knowledge has been opened and it is up to responsible individuals to use this information to improve our collective lives today and in the future. The ethical issues raised by the human genome project can be grouped into two general categories: genetic engineering and genetic information.

Genetic manipulation

The first category consists of issues pertaining to genetic manipulation or what is sometimes called "genetic engineering." The map of the human genome provides information that will allow us to diagnose and eventually treat many diseases. This map will also enable us to determine the genetic basis of numerous physical and psychological traits, which raises the possibility of altering those traits through genetic intervention. Reflection on the ethical permissibility of genetic manipulation is typically structured around two relevant distinctions:

– the distinction between somatic cell and germline intervention, and

– the distinction between therapeutic and enhancement engineering

In germline engineering, changes are passed along in the genome of future generations. Somatic cell manipulation alters body cells, which means that resulting changes are limited to an individual. In contrast, germline manipulation alters reproductive cells, which means that changes are passed on to future generations. Therapeutic engineering occurs when genetic interventions are used to rectify diseases or deficiencies. In contrast, enhancement engineering attempts extend traits or capacities beyond their normal levels.

The use of somatic cell interventions to treat disease is generally regarded as ethically acceptable, because such interventions are consistent with the purpose of medicine, and because risks are localised to a single patient. Germline interventions involve more significant ethical concerns, because risks will extend across generations, magnifying the impact of unforeseen consequences. While these greater risks call for added caution, most ethicists would not object to the use of germline interventions for the treatment of serious disease if we reach the point where such interventions could be performed safely and effectively.

Indeed, germline interventions would be a more efficient method for treating disease, since a single intervention would render both the patient and his or her progeny disease-free, thus removing the need for repeated somatic cell treatments across future generations. Altering one gene may not achieve the desired enhancement since many traits involve a mix of genes. Enhancement engineering is widely regarded as both scientifically and ethically problematic. From a scientific standpoint, it is unlikely that we will soon be able to enhance normally functioning genes without risking grave side effects. For example: Enhancing an individual's height beyond his or her naturally ordained level may inadvertently cause stress to other parts of the organism, such as the heart.

Moreover, many of the traits that might be targeted for enhancement (e.g., intelligence or memory) are genetically multifactorial, and have a strong environmental component. Thus, alteration of single genes would not likely achieve the desired outcome. These problems are magnified, and additional problems arise, when we move from somatic cell enhancements to germline enhancements.

Future generations may feel limited by choices made regarding their genetic traits. In addition to the problem of disseminating unforeseen consequences across generations, we are faced with questions about whether future generations would share their predecessors' views about the desirability of the traits that have been bequeathed to them. Future generations are not likely to be ungrateful if we deprive them of genes associated with horrible diseases, but they may well feel limited by choices we have made regarding their physical, cognitive, or emotional traits. In short, there is a danger that social-historical trends and biases could place genetic limitations on future generations.

Genetic information

The second general category consists of ethical questions pertaining to the acquisition and use of genetic information. Once we pinpoint the genetic basis for diseases and other phenotypic traits, what parameters should be set for the acquisition and use of genetic information? The key issue to be considered here is the use of genetic screening. Screening for diseases with the due consent of a patient or a legal proxy is generally viewed as ethically permissible, but even this form of screening can create some significant ethical challenges. Knowledge that one is or may be affected by a serious disease can create difficult situations for both patients and their families. Consider:

– If a test is positive, what options, medical or otherwise, will be available to ameliorate the condition?

– Will the patient's relatives be informed that they too may be affected by the ailment?

It is the job of genetic counsellors to educate patients about the implications of genetic knowledge, and to help patients anticipate and deal with these challenges. Should mandatory genetic screening be rejected in all situations? Mandatory genetic screening of the adult population raises serious ethical questions about personal liberty and privacy, and thus is not likely to garner widespread support. Nevertheless, we are likely to hear calls for mandatory genetic testing in specific social contexts, and existing practices will no doubt be cited as justifications for such testing.

For example, in the justice system, longstanding practices of fingerprinting, urine testing, and blood testing are already being supplemented by DNA testing. Of particular concern is the specter of genetic testing in the insurance industry. When individuals apply for insurance policies, they are often required to provide family medical history, as well as blood and urine samples. At present, however, insurance companies in the United States cannot require genetic testing of applicants. While this prohibition is designed to prevent genetic discrimination, insurance industry lobbyists will surely be pressing the following kind of argument in coming years: If it is considered fair and proper to identify applicants with high cholesterol and/or a family history of heart disease, and to charge those applicants higher premiums, why should it be considered unfair to utilise genetic testing to accomplish the same goals?

Such questions will have to be seriously considered by ethicists and lawmakers, in the attempt to achieve a fair balance between individual rights and the rights of insurance companies. Indeed, the development of genetic screening for a broad array of diseases and conditions may eventually lead us to rethink the principles that are used to determine insurability and the apportionment of payment burdens. The genetic screening of newborns or others who are incapable of valid consent presents additional ethical questions. Additional ethical questions arise when we consider genetic screening of newborns, young children, and others who cannot give valid consent for such procedures:

– As more genetic tests become available, which ones should be universally administered to newborns?

– What role should parental consent play in determining when children are screened?

Decisions about the implementation of universal genetic screening for newborns will likely follow existing policies, which perform tests for serious, early-onset diseases that are susceptible to treatment. The paradigm case for such universal screening is phenylketonuria (PKU). Newborns are routinely tested for PKU without the explicit consent of parents, under the assumption that parents want to know if their child is afflicted with this potentially devastating but easily treatable condition. Of course, the moral propriety of newborn screening becomes more complicated when we begin to deviate from this paradigm case. Determining whether screening should be pursued in cases like this will not always be easy:

- What if the disease is not easily treatable, or can only be treated at great expense that parents may not want to incur?
- What if an ailment is late onset and untreatable, as is the case with Huntington's disease? What if a test can only determine a probability, not a certainty, that a child will develop a disease?

With genetic testing, there is potential for conflict between a parent's choice and a child's welfare. Of course, from a legal standpoint parents have broad discretion when it comes to decisions about their children's health and welfare, and this will no doubt hold true for decisions about both genetic testing and genetic engineering as these procedures become increasingly available. While this broad discretion is based on respect for parental autonomy and on a desire for minimal government intrusion into family life, we must acknowledge the potential for conflict between a parent's choice and a child's welfare.

- What if a parent refuses to consent to a test that is clearly in their child's best interest?
- What if a parent decides to pursue a genetic "enhancement" that involves significant risks for a child, or that may limit a child's life prospects?

While these questions may seem far-fetched to some, it is worth noting that current laws in most states allow parents to opt out of testing for PKU, despite the fact that this may leave their child exposed to a devastating disease.

Evolutionary Biology Teaching

Evolution is the unifying concept of the biosciences. It is the central organising principle of the historical sciences – biology, geology, and cosmology. Ongoing collection of evidence concerning the details of the process, and elaboration of the theoretical structure that makes the evidence comprehensible, lie at the hub of these sciences. Scientists spend much time debating the details, but there is a consensus as to the overall picture and the basic principles. As in all the sciences, the role of public education is to inform students to a degree that makes it possible for them to understand, at least in general outline, what science and scientists are about. But this is not what happens in some parts of the United States.

Some persons, generally called creationists, perceive the scientific consensus as inimical to their religious beliefs. Creationists have had some degree of success, through political means, in suppressing or distorting the teaching of science in localities of various sizes, ranging from individual classrooms through schools and school districts to entire states. The biological sciences are the arena in which this effort at suppression and distortion has been most visible and by far most extensive. The effects are evident in the kindergarten through high-school science standards of a number of states. In some states, biological evolution is simply ignored, reducing the study of biology in schools from a science to a sort of natural history. In other states, evolution is soft-pedaled, removed from its proper place at the center of biology, represented as a field of hot scientific controversy, or presented in veiled terms.

In many countries the educational system is highly decentralised, with primary authority resting at the local school-board level. Nevertheless, states exercise a significant degree of control over every aspect of education through teacher certification, class-size rules, significant subsidies, and other regulations. With respect to specifically curricular matters, two major instruments of statewide quality control are:

— K-12 standards

— the statewide examinations that are based on them

Given the central place of evolution in the life sciences, what then is required to provide the student with a good understanding of these sciences and the unifying role that evolution plays in them? As with all the sciences, the theoretical framework of biological evolution is somewhat abstract. It does not reveal its power to persons who are not familiar with a reasonable sampling of the broad spectrum of facts that the theory explains and correlates. At the primary grade levels, therefore, standards should focus on those basic facts and ideas of evolution that can later be incorporated into broader perspectives. At the K-3 level, for instance, students should be expected to understand that:

— all living things reproduce

— offspring are similar to but not exactly like their parents

— offspring have to grow up (or change; i.e., metamorphose) before reproducing themselves

— there is a fit between individuals, or species, and their environment (e.g., terrestrial, aquatic, a

— the earth is over 4 billion years old, allowing much time for biological as well as geological evolution

The theory and principles of evolution should be examined at higher grades. At higher grade levels, these ideas can be supplemented by an understanding of:

— the nature of competition for survival between and within species

- the consequence that not all offspring live long enough to reproduce
- the limitation imposed on the number of offspring that survive by such environmental factors as availability of food and water; predators, and temperature
- the variability among individuals that leads to differential survivability in a particular environment
- the specialisation of species to fit ecological niches and the impact of environmental change on the tenability of those niches
- the underlying role of genetic variation that results from both sexual reproduction and random mutation
- the nonrandom way that natural selection operates on the existing population in spite of the many random factors that determine the survival of any individual

Lessons should emphasise the link between geological and biological evolution. At the middle and high school levels, these ideas can be unified, and such concepts as Mendel's laws, genetic drift, sexual selection, and other significant mechanisms can be introduced. Coevolution, commensalism, and the complex interactions of ecosystems are important applications of the basic concepts. The magnitude of the geological/evolutionary time scale is so different from the time scales of everyday life that it is difficult to grasp, and must be introduced with care.

The fact that the same general time scale underlies both geological and biological evolution is an important link between the two sciences. Parallel to these macroscopic concepts, the underlying microscopic mechanisms must be introduced at suitable high school grade levels. These include:

- the relation of genotype to phenotype
- DNA as an information carrier
- the expression of DNA in protein synthesis
- the implications thereof at the various levels of organisation from organelles through cells, tissues, organs, and individual organisms, to populations
- the identification of Mendel's and Morgan's abstract gene as a sequence of bases in a DNA molecule, a dramatic triumph of the biological sciences
- the origin of mitochondria and chloroplasts in prokaryotes parasitic on eukaryotes
- the special roles of mitochondrial and Y-chromosome DNA in tracing single-sex ancestral lines

Evolution is a big picture concept, from the history of the universe to its smallest genetic component. It is also important to introduce, at the proper time, the understanding that biological evolution does not take place in a vacuum. The biota of the earth coexist with the nonliving parts of the earth, and each influences the other. Therefore, the facts and, subsequently, the theoretical structure of geological evolution must be introduced concurrently with biological evolution. Similarly, the earth is part of the solar system and the solar system is part of a hierarchy of still larger structures, up to the universe as a whole. The student should be empowered to view the history of the universe, from the general cosmological picture down to the smaller scales characterising the earth and its smaller elements, as a seamless whole.

Evolution Theory

Evolution theory explains how organisms have changed

over time. Scientific understanding requires both facts and theories that can explain those facts in a coherent manner. Evolution, in this context, is both a fact and a theory. It is an incontrovertible fact that organisms have changed, or evolved, during the history of life on Earth. And biologists have identified and investigated mechanisms that can explain the major patterns of change. The field of evolutionary biology seeks to provide explanations for four conspicuous patterns that are manifest in nature. The first three concern living species, whereas the fourth relates to fossils.

Genes are linked to how organisms look and behave. Genetic variation. There is tremendous genetic diversity within almost all species, including humans. No two individuals have the same DNA sequence, with the exception of identical twins or clones. This genetic variation contributes to phenotypic variation—that is, diversity in the outward appearance and behaviour of individuals of the same species. Organisms must adapt to their environment to survive.

Adaptation: Living organisms have morphological, biochemical, and behavioural features that make them well adapted for life in the environments in which they are usually found. For example, consider the hollow bones and feathers of birds that enable them to fly, or the cryptic coloration that allows many organisms to hide from their predators. These features may give the superficial appearance that organisms were designed by a creator (or engineer) to live in a particular environment. Evolutionary biology has demonstrated that adaptations arise through selection acting on genetic variation. Species evolved along different paths from a common ancestor.

Divergence: All living species differ from one another. In some cases, these differences are subtle, while in other cases the differences are dramatic. Carl Linnaeus proposed a classification that is still used today with slight changes. In the modern scheme, similar species are grouped into genera, similar genera into families, and so on. This hierarchical pattern of relationship produces a tree-like pattern, which implies a process of splitting and divergence from a common ancestor. Fossils provide evidence of evolutionary changes.

Fossil species: Fossils are the mineralised remnants or impressions of once-living organisms. Many fossils, such as trilobites and dinosaurs, belong to groups that no longer exist on the face of the Earth. Conversely, many modern species appear similar to other fossils, yet fossils of the modern species are absent from rocks of corresponding ages. The age of the Earth is estimated to be about 4.5 billion years, with the earliest bacterial fossils about 3.5 billion years old. Fossils from around 550 million years ago (the Cambrian period) show a diverse assemblage of multicellular animals.

Evolutionary biology provides a scientific framework for understanding the changes that have occurred since the first life forms arose on Earth several billion years ago. Biochemists, geologists, and physicists seek natural explanations for the origin of life on Earth. While progress has been made in this area, the origin of life remains an interesting, but unanswered, question.

Biological evolution results from changes over time in the genetic constitution of species. Genetic changes often, but not always, produce noticeable changes in the appearance or behaviour of organisms. Evolution requires both the production of variation and the spread of some variants that replace others. Genetic variation arises through two processes, mutation and recombination. Mutation occurs when DNA is imperfectly copied during replication, leading to a difference between a parent's gene and that of its offspring. Some mutations affect only one bit in the DNA; others produce rearrangements of large blocks of DNA.

Recombination occurs when genes from two parents are shuffled to produce an offspring, as happens regularly in sexual reproduction. Usually the two parents belong to the same species, but sometimes (especially in bacteria) genes move between more distantly related organisms. The fate of any particular genetic variant depends on two processes, drift and selection. Drift refers to random fluctuations in gene frequency, and its effects are usually seen at the level of DNA. Ten flips of a coin do not always produce exactly five heads and five tails; drift refers to the same statistical issue applied to the transmission of genetic variants across generations.

Natural selection guarantees that the fittest will pass on their genes. The principle of natural selection was discovered by Charles Darwin and it is the process by which organisms become adapted to their environments. Selection occurs when some individual organisms have genes that encode physical or behavioural features that allow them to better harvest resources, avoid predators, and such relative to other individuals that do not carry the same genes. The individuals that have these useful features will tend to leave more offspring than other individuals, so the responsible genes will become more common over time, leading the population as a whole to become better adapted. Distinct species diverge from one ancestor and can no longer interbreed.

The process that many people find most confusing about evolution is speciation, which is not a separate mechanism at all, but rather a consequence of the preceding mechanisms played out in time and space. Speciation occurs when a population changes sufficiently over time that it becomes convenient to refer to the early and late forms by different names. Speciation also occurs when one population splits into two distinct forms that can no longer interbreed. Reproductive isolation does not generally happen in one generation; it may require many thousands of generations when, for example, one part of a population becomes geographically separated from the rest and adapts to a new environment. Given time, it is inevitable that two populations that live apart will diverge by mutation, drift, and selection until eventually their genes are no longer compatible for successful reproduction.

Evidence for Evolution

Evidence from Fossils: Fossils are the most easily observed evidence for evolution. Evidence from fossils. Based on myriad similarities and differences between living species, evolutionary biology makes predictions about the features of ancestral forms. For example, numerous features indicate that birds are derived from reptilian ancestors. By contrast, these data reject the possibility that birds were derived from other groups, such as flying insects. Scientists have discovered fossil birds with feathers and legs like modern birds, but which also have teeth, clawed digits on their forelimbs, and a tailbone like their reptilian ancestors. Fossils are especially important evidence for evolution because, with little effort, each of us can use our eyes and minds to observe and interpret the dinosaur and other ancient fossils in public museums.

Evidence from genetics. The genomes of all organisms contain overwhelming evidence for evolution. All living species share the same basic mechanism of heredity using

DNA (or RNA in some viruses) to encode genes that are passed from parent to offspring, and which are transcribed and translated into proteins during each organism's life. Using DNA sequences, biologists quantify the genetic similarities and differences among species, in order to determine which species are more closely related to one another and which are more distantly related. In doing so, biologists use essentially the same evidence and logic used to determine paternity in lawsuits.

The pattern of genetic relatedness between all species indicates a branching tree that implies divergence from a common ancestor. Within this tree of life, there are also occasional reticulations where two branches fuse, rather than separate. The genetic similarity between species, which exists by virtue of evolution from the same ancestral form, is an essential fact that underlies biomedical research. This similarity allows us to begin to understand the effects of our own genes by conducting research on genes from other species. For example, genes that control the process of DNA repair in bacteria, flies, and mice have been discovered to influence certain cancers in humans. These findings also suggest strategies for intervention that can be explored in other species before testing on humans. Evolution is evident today in how bacteria evolve to resist antibiotics.

Evolution in action: Evolutionary change continues to this day, and it will proceed so long as life itself exists. In recent years, many bacterial pathogens have evolved resistance to antibiotics used to cure infections, thereby requiring the development of new and more costly treatments. In some frightening cases, bacteria have evolved resistance to every available antibiotic, so there is no longer any effective treatment. In the case of HIV, which causes AIDS, significant viral evolution occurs within the course of infection of a single patient, and this rapid evolution enables the virus to evade the immune system.

Many agricultural pests have evolved resistance to chemicals that farmers have used for only a few decades. As we work to control diseases and pests, the responsible organisms have been evolving to escape our controls. Moreover, scientists can perform experiments to study evolution in real time, just as experiments are used to observe dynamic processes in physics, chemistry, and other branches of biology. To study evolution in action, scientists use organisms like bacteria and fruitflies that reproduce quickly, so they can see changes that require many generations.

Evolutionary biology is misunderstood by some people. It has an image problem. Some people are threatened by it and thus oppose it. Many people – even many of its defenders – view evolutionary biology as irrelevant outside of academia. And in a few cases, even though evolution is perceived as relevant, some see it as responsible for death and misfortune, e.g., drug-resistance in medicine and pesticide-resistance in agriculture. Most people are unaware of uses of evolutionary biology. Public non-appreciation of evolutionary biology may depend as much on its perceived irrelevance as anything else.

Yet, evolution, especially microevolution, has been fundamental to some social improvements this century, and it promises to be profoundly important to biomedical technology in the next generation. For example: Evolution underlies many improvements in agriculture (e.g., the artificial selection of crop strains and livestock breeds). A less well-known fact is that evolutionary principles were used to produce many of our best vaccines and that evolution also causes problems with the use of some of those vaccines. Some of the most promising areas for the future use of evolutionary biology lie in drug development and the biotechnology industry; patents worth vast amounts of money are based on ways of creating evolution (or avoiding evolution) in test tubes.

Polio vaccine is an old example but it is a good one. The vaccine now used to immunise against the disease poliomyelitis is a live poliovirus that we eat. This live virus does not give us the disease (except to about 1-2 in a million people vaccinated) because it is genetically weakened so that our body can defeat it. This process of weakening is called attenuation, and it is an evolutionary process. The attenuated vaccine strains came from wild, virulent strains of poliovirus, but they were evolved by Albert Sabin to become attenuated. Essentially, he grew the viruses outside of humans, and as the viruses became adapted to those non-human conditions, they lost their ability to cause disease in people. Evolution can also destroy the effects of vaccine. This method of attenuation has been used to create many live vaccines.

Evolution was the good guy here because it helped us make the vaccine. But the role of evolution and evolutionary biology does not end here – evolution becomes the bad guy too. When a person eats the attenuated virus, it infects his/her gut cells and starts doing what viruses do – making copies of itself. These viral progeny infect other cells in your gut, those in turn make other viral progeny, and so on, until you have a population of poliovirus growing inside your gut. Some of these viruses carry mutations, and some of those mutations (one or two in particular) restore most of the virulence to the virus.

In your gut, these restored viruses may have a selective advantage over the weakened viruses, and in the course of a week or so after eating the vaccine, you begin shedding virus with restored virulence. In short, an evolutionary process inside your gut undoes Albert Sabin's attenuation of the virus. Understanding evolution gives us clues on how to vaccinate effectively. These restored viruses do not hurt the person taking the vaccine because by the time restored viruses get to be abundant in the gut, the immune system has enough of a head start to keep the virus from getting into the central nervous system. Disease is caused only if the virus gets into the central nervous system. However, if we were to vaccinate just one person in a population of non-immunised people the restored viruses shed from this one person would infect other people and could start an epidemic of nasty poliovirus.

In fact, people have gotten the disease from people who were recently vaccinated. Fortunately, this problem caused by evolution has an easy solution – when polio vaccine is first introduced to a community, we try to vaccinate everyone in the community at once. This is what happened in the U.S. when the Sabin vaccine was first introduced in the U.S. in the 1950's (vaccine "Sundays"), and it was done in other countries as well. The WHO did all of China in 3 days, and vaccinated 90,000,000 people in India in one day. Thus, understanding the evolution of poliovirus virulence allows us to use the vaccine without causing unnecessary disease.

The evolution of drug resistance in bacteria is one of the simplest examples of evolution that we have. It is extremely relevant to medicine. And since it is a case of microevolution, it is an example that should be widely embraced. Yet many people profoundly misunderstand drug resistance. Even news reports from the BBC have gotten it wrong. Bacterial resistance to antibiotics is an evolutionary phenomenon:

– heavy use of antibiotics selects bacteria that are genetically resistant to the drug

– with continued use of antibiotics, those resistant forms of the bacteria multiply and spread to other hosts

– eventually, resistant bacteria replace the population of once-sensitive bacteria.

• In the minds of some people, however, the problem with misuse of antibiotics is that it can lead to a physiological tolerance in the person taking the drugs, so that antibiotics are no longer effective in that person. That is, they think that drugs become ineffective because of the person, not the bacterium. This erroneous, non-evolutionary view has serious ramifications, because it can lead to an unwarranted complacency about antibiotic misuse. Because drug resistance is evolutionary, your neighbour's misuse of antibiotics can injure or kill you. The unregulated use of antibiotics in, say, Europe can bring strains for which we have no defense to the U.S. and our hospitals.

It is not simply a matter of the proper use of antibiotics in each of us individually; it is a matter of everyone's proper use of antibiotics. It is tempting to speculate that the common, though not universal, public failure to understand the evolutionary basis of drug resistance reflects a widespread ignorance of evolutionary principles, even principles professed to be uncontroversial. The fact that this misunderstanding is not confined to the western side of the Atlantic suggests that political opposition to the teaching of evolution is not the only cause. Why do creationists object to these ideas? The extrascientific pressures against the teaching of biological evolution are diverse.

However, they manifest themselves mainly in three major classes of objections, which correspond to the following factual and theoretical implications of biological evolution:

- To achieve the diversity of life we observe today, the evolutionary process has required several billion years.
- All living things, humans not excepted, are descended from common ancestors.

  The evolutionary process is a natural one susceptible to scientific investigation and thus by definition cannot include supernatural intervention as a necessary component.

A minority of religious fundamentalists believes the earth is about 10,000 years old. The first of these premises conflicts with a particular interpretation of the first few chapters of the Book of Genesis. According to this interpretation, the universe is less than a millionth as old as the scientific evidence implies — that is, a few thousand years rather than some tens of billions. This particular interpretation of Genesis, generally called young-earth creationism, is held mainly by a subset of evangelical Protestants and some ultra-orthodox Jews and Muslims. Young-earth creationists fear that the several alternative interpretations of Genesis supported by most Christians and Jews undermine the entire authority of the Bible.

The second premise is objected to by young-earthers and some others who hold that humankind has a special, divinely ordained place in the universe and is the central concern of the divinity. According to this belief, God could not have lumped humans (for whose benefit He created the universe and everything in it) with mere animals, let alone other living things. Such believers hold, moreover, that teaching the biological relationship of humans to other animals inevitably undermines any possible moral or ethical teaching. The third premise is the special province of a class of anti-evolutionists called intelligent-design or irreducible-complexity advocates. These persons have revived a position set forth in the 17th century by John Ray and just after 1800 by William Paley.

Specifically, they dust off the view that living beings are too complicated to have evolved, and that their creation by an intelligent (read as divine) designer is just the entrée into the natural world that God requires if we are to believe in Him. Other pressure groups object to evolution as well, on various grounds and from political perspectives that range from right to left or are not classifiable politically. However, the views described above, held mainly by a subset of Protestant evangelicals, have by far the greatest impact on public education.

Applications of Evolutionary Biology

There are numerous ways to apply evolutionary biology to our needs today, among them:

- prolonging the life of drug/chemical resistant compounds
- constructing evolutionary trees
- pathogen tracking
- industrial production of biochemicals and other agents

Drug resistance and chemical resistance in microbes, plants, and animals: In the latter half of this century, industry has been exceptionally good at providing compounds to kill viruses, bacteria, insects that eat crops and weeds that grow in crop fields. We even have an abundance of chemotherapy drugs to kill rogue cancer cells. Yet virtually without exception, our attempts to kill these organisms cause them to evolve resistance against the chemicals used to kill them. For example:

- Isolates of the AIDS virus with up to 15 different drug-resistance mutations are known, and the latest drugs are becoming ineffective.
- Some strains of bacteria are resistant to all available antibiotics.
- For multi-drug resistant tuberculosis, surgery is the only cure because antibiotics don't work and only 50% of those infected survive.
- Chemotherapy for cancer often fails because drug-resistant cells evolve during treatment.
- Pesticide resistance and herbicide resistance is so common now that the financial incentive to make new pesticides and herbicides is break-even or worse.

Evolutionary biology suggests how best to prolong the useful life of drugs/chemicals. The amounts of chemicals used, what combinations of chemicals to use, and when to apply them are all questions that can be assessed from the perspective of preventing or slowing the evolution of resistance. In some cases now, the companies marketing the compounds have a financial interest in maintaining the longevity of their product, and they are funding studies by evolutionary biologists to develop wise use protocols. In other cases, however, economic and emotional forces dictate policies that speed up the evolution of resistance (e.g., patients demand and physicians write prescriptions for antibiotics for viral infections; antibiotics are used in animal feed).

Evolutionary trees: Perhaps the core of evolutionary theory is that all life forms are connected to each other through common ancestry. Molecular biology has reinforced this view to a far greater level than was deemed possible even 50 years ago. On a short time scale, of course, we observe that this is true – everything alive comes from something else that is both alive and similar. One of the big developments in evolutionary biology over the last 2 decades is a methodology to estimate the underlying patterns of ancestry among living things. These reconstructions of evolutionary history are known as phylogenies, or phylogenetic trees, because they are branched somewhat like trees when drawn from bottom to top. We can use molecular data to estimate the common ancestries of life as far back as we like – for example, between bacteria and our mitochondria (the energy-producing organelles in our cells). But we can also use these methods to estimate much more recent ancestries. And these methods have found many worthy uses in tracking infectious diseases.

Molecular Epidemiology: To an epidemiologist studying infectious diseases, it is very useful to know how or where a person became infected with the disease. This information is perhaps the most basic fact we can use in preventing the further spread of a disease. For over a decade now, epidemiologists have been using DNA sequences of viruses to make phylogenetic trees and thereby track the sources of infections. Some of these examples are spectacular. In a highly publicised case in Lafayette, Louisiana in 1998, a woman claimed that her ex-lover (a physician) deliberately injected her with HIV-tainted blood (HIV is the virus that causes AIDS). There were no records of her injection and no witnesses. So how could her story be tested? Evolutionary trees provide the best scientific evidence in a case like this.

If one person gives the virus to another, there are few differences between the virus in the donor and the virus in the recipient. As the virus goes from person to person, it keeps changing and gets more and more different over time. Thus, the HIV sequences in two individuals who got the virus from two different people will be very different. Thus, if the woman's story were true, her virus should be very similar to the virus in the person whose blood was drawn but should be very different from viruses taken from other people in Lafayette. That was exactly what the evolutionary trees showed; her virus appeared to have come from the patient's virus but was unlike the virus taken from other people in town. Since there was no way to explain how she would have gotten that patient's virus on her own, the evolutionary analysis supported her story.

Evolutionary trees have been used in many other cases of infectious disease transmission:

- the transmission of the AIDS virus by a dentist to his patients
- deer mice as the source of hantavirus infections in the Four-Corners area
- the source of rabies viruses in human cases, leading to the discovery of a case in which rabies virus took at least 7 years to kill a person
- whether recent cases of polio in North America were relict strains from the New World, were vaccine strains, or were introduced from Asia

4. Industrial production of biochemicals and other agents

"Directed evolution", i.e. artificially-induced evolution, has become part of the jargon in biotechnology:

- Artificially evolved enzymes and other proteins are soon to become part of household and medical technologies.
- We will have protein-based drugs that, unlike the proteins inside our bodies, degrade slowly so that we don't need to take so much of them.
- Ensymes are being evolved to work in detergents (which they don't normally do).
- And as the stuff of futuristic novels, molecules are being developed to bind anthrax spores, ricin molecules, and other potential bioterrorism agents.

All of these developments take advantage of one or more forms of test-tube evolution. Armed with a knowledge of how natural selection works and combined with the right kinds of laboratory technology, people can create molecules to perform seemingly any kind of function. In some of the more spectacular cases, these test tube evolution methods have created enzymes from purely random pools of DNA (or RNA) sequences. Even 10 years ago, it was thought that a DNA enzyme was impossible, yet armed with only an understanding of how to apply test tube evolution, a DNA enzyme can now be created in days. The pace of evolutionary biology and its ramifications has outstripped public awareness as well as expanded beyond the knowledge base of most classical evolutionary biologists. Even the textbooks have not kept up. It is thus difficult but important to recognise that evolutionary biology has implications to a new century of medicine, agriculture, biotechnology, and even law.

Students educated with this knowledge will have an edge in the competitive job markets of the future, but at least in some areas of medicine, a basic public understanding of evolutionary principles may be essential in successfully waging the ongoing war with infectious diseases. The public education system is based on the concept of local control with limited oversight from the state. One may characterise public school governance as a modified diffuse democracy. In democracies, decisions are made by majority rule. Citizens vote with equal voice on the basis of their opinions, regardless of what those opinions are or how strongly founded in fact they may be.

We believe, of course, that a well-educated electorate is an essential basis for workable democracy, and this has always been a cardinal argument for public education. But democracy cannot permeate all aspects of every social institution. It is certainly not consistent with the education process itself. Education cannot be democratic because the teacher directly supervises the progress of the students, using his or her superior knowledge and adhering to standards imposed from levels above the classroom.

Science is not democratic, either. In a democratic society, citizens who do not like the existing state of affairs can change it. This has happened often. But nature is not so flexible. We may find Newton's second law of motion contrary to common sense because it links acceleration, rather than velocity, to applied force. But we cannot change this; what we can do is learn how to manipulate it. We may believe it an insult to human dignity that the earth is not at the center of the universe but we cannot move it there. We may find moral or aesthetic objections to the manner in which natural history unfolds but we cannot command nature to take another course.

Science is also undemocratic in the social sense, i.e., those who do not have the scientist's special knowledge, skills, and experience cannot have equal voice in achieving a scientific consensus concerning a class of phenomena. The public school has no authority to impose opinions on its students. But it has the duty to explain to them the consensus of scientists on any particular issue, and the methodology by which scientists proceed to discover new knowledge and merge it into that consensus.

Biological evolution is just one of the most important of many broad issues on which substantially all working scientists agree. There may be a few persons with scientific credentials who disagree, but they do not contribute to the progress that is the hallmark of science. It is not simply that these dissenters are wrong, because wrong answers can sometimes stimulate controversy that helps lead to correct answers. Rather, as the physicist Wolfgang Pauli liked to say, they are not even wrong. That is, their arguments are useless and even detrimental to the pursuit of further knowledge.

Teaching Bioethics

Bioethics is an important consideration for teachers because students:

- want to know about the world around them
- are experiencing self-discovery, which includes questioning issues
- need to hone their critical thinking skills

Scientists from the human genome project predict that we will determine the genetic causes of human disease long before treatments are available. Access to genetic and sequence maps will alter the face of clinical medicine in the twenty-first century. With the gap between our ability to diagnose and treat or cure genetic diseases ranging from five to twenty or more years, coupled with the high economic and social costs of disease, there is increasing pressure to explore genetic manipulation of somatic cells. How do we decide among current scientifically available options? How do we make those difficult ethical choices?

Adolescents are passionately interested in ethical questions suggesting adolescence may be a critical period for including bioethics in science education. Knowledge arises when the mind interacts with content; an understanding of ethical issues develops as an evolving process around real-life situations. The question is what role should teachers play in the acquisition of this knowledge? Plato asked a form of this question more than two thousand years ago: Is ethics taught, inherited or passed on by some other mechanism? Does ethics need to be taught? Experts have studied how we learn ethical concepts and behaviour and what roles nature and nurture play in the process. Their hypotheses don't always agree.

Nature is More Influential than Nurture: Can the mind actually build knowledge from sensory information? We instinctively know some things, although group interactions and environmental factors may modify this knowledge. For example, as an extension of the mother-infant bond, we learn kinship preferences, recognition of specific individuals, social communication, and long term infant care. Some scientific studies support this view. For example, neurologist Oliver Sacks befriended a young boy named Stephen, an autistic savant who was capable of memorising complex scenery at a glance and retaining the information for long periods of time. From an early age he appeared to have little need for nurture – human or otherwise.

Nurture is More Onfluential than Nature: Leading a field of neurobiologists, who explore how the human brain learns about the world, Nobel Laureate Gerald Edelman hypothesizes that with repeated experiences, we develop and reinforce anatomically based concept maps. These concept maps subsequently modify how sensory information is processed and organised. "Natural Law" ethics, which has been traced to the writings of Aristotle and Plato, states that decision-making principles can be discovered through careful reflection and by observing nature. The law of nature, rather than individual preferences, determines what actions are right. The human mind need only possess the capacity for reasoned thought and the ability to communicate.

Nature and Nurture Interact in Sequential Stages: In a series of elegantly designed experiments, child psychologist Jean Piaget proposed that children pass through developmental stages where one stage builds on an earlier stage through assimilation and accommodation to the real world. Psychologist Lawrence Kohlberg strongly believed that moral development occurs in six stages. We grow from a point of self-interest to one of an increasingly larger circle of people. Our perspective changes with age and is comparable to growth in areas of psychological development. Educators should note that educational psychologist Carol Gilligan, Kolberg's student, criticises his theory because it is based on studies of males and, therefore, contains a significant gender bias. Others have also criticised Kohlberg for placing a higher value on one form of moral reasoning over another.

The acquisition of ethics and other forms of knowledge are dependent on exposure to content, properly timed experiences, and practice with reasoning skills. Since we acquire this knowledge from heritable and external sources, such as the classroom, students need an opportunity to:

- engage in discussions that allow them to examine their values
- practice resolving ethical conflicts in a real world context.

Bioethics in Medical Education

During the past decade, biomedical ethics (commonly called bioethics) has become a popular topic for media coverage. This is largely due to increased complexity of caring for patients and the difficult decisions that new technologies demand. Examples include high-visibility issues like the completion of the human genome project, cloning, patenting of human tissue products, and transplants. However, doctors worry (or should worry) more often about less visible but more common issues such as ensuring patient self-determination and proper informed consent for medical procedures, end-of-life decision making, research ethics, reproductive medicine, and managed care and related economic issues. Despite the trendy nature of cloning and other hot issues, there are numerous ways in which the knowledge that practicing physicians have about medical ethics and law can have a more direct impact on the type and quality of care that the average patient receives.

In order to provide medical care in an ethical and humane way, physicians need to be better educated about specific aspects of ethical medical practice and learn to think critically about the increasingly complex world of medical practice. Routine bioethics education for medical students and resident physicians, and continuing medical education for practicing doctors, are the best ways to accomplish this goal. It is vital that physicians understand basic aspects of law and the legal system in order to practice good medicine. This means that knowledge of law has profound ethical implications for patient care and well-being.

Physicians know substantially less about medical law when they get such legal information from other physicians. This is not to suggest that all physicians are ignorant of relevant law but rather, that there is great variability among physicians in knowledge of law (and ethics). Thus bioethicists, who are trained in specific aspects of medical law (and who may themselves be physicians), are appropriate persons to supplement physicians' knowledge in this area. Other research has demonstrated that how people think about risk (like the risk of malpractice lawsuits) affects the way they react to it, creating ethical consequences. Because risk management is an issue that concerns most physicians, improving doctors' knowledge of medical law can help them better understand and estimate risks, as well as learn where they may be unconsciously overestimating certain risks in ways that have negative effects for patient care. Thus, law and ethics are inevitably intertwined in clinical medicine.

Knowledge of the health care delivery system is vital. Understanding social and institutional aspects of health care delivery is also vital. Doctors should know how hospitals and other medical institutions function and how different health care providers and administrators work together. These relationships include physicians' interactions with nurses, respiratory therapists, physical therapists, occupational therapists, nurses' aides, and members of hospital administration in the areas of finance and risk management. Bioethicists can assist physicians-in-training to understand how such institutional relationships may function differently from those to which they are accustomed and help them assimilate to new institutional structures. Good physician-role-models also play a significant part in this process.

Bioethicists can teach doctors and students about clinical ethics. Practical application of bioethics concepts is essential for the well-being of both patients and physicians. The integration of bioethics into clinical medicine through the practice of "clinical ethics" is a major part of many bioethicists' jobs. This usually occurs in at least two ways, first by educating physicians-in-training, and second, by conducting clinical ethics consultations, which have both an educational role and are designed to assist with a particular ethical problem in a clinical setting. In this setting, the bioethicist provides services that assist specific patients and their families, as well as health care providers.

By modelling good clinical ethics practice, bioethicists can teach physicians ways to better perform these functions. Physicians should be aware of current health policies and legislation. Understanding health policy and the legislative process is an important part of delivering good health care in the modern world. Some good examples of issues from the realm of health policy, of which physicians should be aware, include: state and federal regulation of health care financing; public health and health promotion efforts; legislative action on end-of-life decisions and pain control; pharmaceutical regulation; and the impact of emerging genetic testing and other biotechnology. Physicians having a strong interest in one or more of these issues may wish to become active in advocating a particular piece of legislation or other policy. Because many physicians do not ordinarily think in these terms, bioethicists can make them aware of ways that health care providers can become more active in the public policy process.

Bioethicists can also introduce physicians to medical humanities. Knowledge and experience of the humanities is a key element of caring for patients as persons. For example when physicians read poetry or fiction that explores aspects of human illness and suffering, it provides them with exposure to the human experience of health care that may become lost in the daily activities of technological medicine. The humanities can thus add to the richness of both patients' and physicians' experiences. Many bioethicists are trained in particular disciplines of the humanities, and some bioethicists have specific training in "medical humanities." Thus, the bioethicist is the ideal person to provide such background for aspiring physicians.

Physicians should be wary of conflict-of-interest situations. With academic medicine becoming ever more dependent on the private sector in health care, the ability to think critically about ethical issues and take appropriate action in response is a key element of academic physicians' work. A good example is the increasing impact of conflicts of interest. As research physicians increasingly have a direct financial interest in the outcome of their research, bioethicists can provide a sensitivity to the public perceptions that may emerge from such financial relationships. Critical thinking is the stock-in-trade of bioethicists and they can foster it in many ways with physicians.

Bioethicists are generally trained in philosophical ethics and law, as well as the social sciences and humanities. However, the level and type of training among individuals varies to a significant extent, so physicians seeking bioethics consultations should be aware of the particular type of expertise they need and search out a bioethicist with proper background when possible. Bioethicists can provide a more objective and balanced view of complex ethical issues in health care settings. In other words, bioethicists can often provide an outside perspective on medical care. However, as bioethics practice becomes a more routine part of medicine there is a danger of bioethicists being co-opted by the system they are charged with improving. For this reason, bioethicists should be scrupulous in maintaining their objectivity where possible.

Many bioethicists have extensive experience in analysing and resolving actual dilemmas in clinical medicine. In fact, "clinical ethics" has become an unofficial sub-specialty of the field. Educational efforts specifically targeted to teach bioethics issues to physicians are effective. Recent research suggests that after a course in bioethics, physicians have a more subtle understanding of ethical issues and are better able to analyse relevant issues critically. What is a good example of the ways that these factors converge?

An excellent example of the importance of all these factors is the ongoing debate over control of severe pain in terminally ill patients. First, because of the risk of diversion of narcotic medications into illegal markets, there are strong legal restrictions placed on prescribing of these drugs. Fear of overly-sealous government enforcement of these laws may cause many physicians to err on the side of caution and prescribe lower doses of these medications than necessary to relieve patients' pain. Thus, regulations affecting pain relief medication can have unintended consequences of diminishing patients' ability to obtain legitimate relief. Improved legal knowledge among physicians may reduce fear and misunderstanding and may increase prescribing of appropriate levels of medication for pain relief. However, knowledge of these unintended effects is also necessary among policy makers and legislators.

The misnamed Pain Relief Promotion Act of 1999 is but one example of how policy and medical care may collide in ways that have negative effects on patient care. This recently-proposed bill was designed to override the physician-assisted suicide law currently in effect in Oregon and to prohibit other states from enacting similar laws. Expert bioethicists believe that if this bill were to pass, palliative care could be compromised due to the fear of criminal prosecution of physicians. Thus, physicians concerned about being able to prescribe appropriate pain control for their dying patients should take an active role in the legislative and process to ensure that patients' interests are upheld. As part of this effort, physicians could be active in public education about the impact of such legislation as well as contacting legislators directly to voice the concerns of the health care community and make clear the possible unintended consequences.

Finally, but not least in importance, viewing cases through the lens of medical humanities can better enable physicians to understand their patients' experience of pain and alleviate suffering to the extent possible. Thus, legal, social, institutional, policy, and humanistic factors all play a role in such analysis.

The most critical barrier to achieving uniform bioethics education in the medical curriculum is financial constraints. Most bioethics programmes in medical schools are not funded in a way that ensures their continuation. Instead, bioethics programmes usually depend on funds set aside by the dean or other discretionary sources such as federal grants that could rapidly dry up. The source of such discretionary funds is overhead money from scientific grants. For example, when the department of biochemistry receives a grant from the National Institutes of Health some of the overhead money from that grant may be used to benefit bioethics programme. The risk in this approach is that bioethics may come to be viewed as marginal to the mission of the medical school and therefore expendable. Bioethics curricula lack national standards.

Another barrier to bioethics implementation throughout medical curricula is that there remains substantial variation in the quantity and quality of curriculum. Because the field is fairly new and remains underfunded, less effort has been expended in developing programmes than in other aspects of medical education. However, the proliferation of graduate programmes awarding Ph.D.s in bioethics means there will soon be a good supply of well trained persons able to fill this gap. Bioethics courses are often meager in content. Another barrier is giving bioethics lip service but not substance. Although accrediting organisations require institutions to address ethics issues to some extent, the compliance bar is set fairly low. Institutions with ethics programmes that only satisfy the minimum requirement of accrediting agencies do not have adequate services to ensure ethical patient care.

Physicians who are mentors and teachers must indicate to students and trainees that ethics is an crucial part of what they are learning. This message must permeate the educational environment. In all these efforts, however, the role of the bioethicist should be one of a colleague possessing specialised knowledge and skills, who is working with doctors, rather than an outside professional seeking to monitor physician behaviour. Patient care may suffer if physicians are not educated about bioethical issues. The most important implication of these barriers is for patient well-being.

If young physicians are not taught the importance of bioethics issues for their clinical practice, patients may suffer needless pain, their legal rights of self-determination may be disregarded, and their experience of health care will be less than optimal. If this is to be avoided, bioethics must receive a higher priority in medical education in the future than it has occupied in the past.

Bibliography

Beyer, Landon E.and others, *Preparing Teachers as Professionals*, New York: Teachers College Press, 1989.

Broderick, Maria, editor, *For Teachers about Teaching*, Cambridge: Harvard Educational Review, 1988.

Bullough, Robert V., *First-Year Teacher: a Case Study*, New York: Teachers College Press, 1989.

Burke, Peter, *Teacher Development: Induction, Renewal, and Redirection*, New York: Falmer Press, 1987.

Darling-Hammond, Linda, editor, *Professional Development Schools: Schools for Developing a Profession*, New York: Teachers, College Press, 1994.

Dollase, Richard H., *Voices of Beginning Teachers: Visions and Realities*, New York: Teachers College Press, 1992.

Dunkin, Michael J., *International Encyclopedia of Teaching and Teacher Education*, Oxford: Pergamon Press, 1987.

Phillips, Charles E., *College of Education*, Toronto: Memories of OCE. Toronto: University of Toronto, Faculty of Education, Guidance Centre, 1977.

Ontario College of Teachers, *College calls on Ministry to fund additional teacher training spaces immediately*, Professionally Speaking, June 1999.

_______________, "Standards of Practice for the Teaching Profession", Toronto: OCT, 1998.

_______________, *Privilege of Professionalism*, Toronto: OCT, 1995.

Reavis, Charles A., *Teacher Improvement Through Clinical Supervision*, Bloomington, Indiana: Phi Delta Kappa Educational Foundation, 1978.

University of Toronto, *College of Education*, Program Committee, Focus: Report on Future Programs of Teacher Education, University of Toronto, September 1971 and Refocus: Responses to Focus, 1971-1972.

Index